P9-DEO-991

ANALYZING & INTERPRETING ETHNOGRAPHIC DATA

ETHNOGRAPHER'S TOOLKIT

Edited by Jean J. Schensul, *Institute for Community Research, Hartford*, and
Margaret D. LeCompte, *School of Education, University of Colorado, Boulder*

The **Ethnographer's Toolkit** is designed with you, the novice fieldworker, in mind. In a series of seven brief books, the editors and authors of the Toolkit take you through the multiple, complex steps of doing ethnographic research in simple, reader-friendly language. Case studies, checklists, key points to remember, and additional resources to consult, are all included to help the reader fully understand the ethnographic process. Eschewing a step-by-step formula approach, the authors are able to explain the complicated tasks and relationships that occur in the field in clear, helpful ways. Research designs, data collection techniques, analytical strategies, research collaborations, and an array of uses for ethnographic work in policy, programming, and practice, are described in the volumes. The **Toolkit** is the perfect starting point for professionals in diverse professional fields including social welfare, education, health, economic development, and the arts, as well as for students and experienced researchers unfamiliar with the demands of conducting good ethnography.

Summer 1999/ 7 volumes/ paperback boxed set/ 0-7619-9042-9

BOOKS IN THE ETHNOGRAPHER'S TOOLKIT

ANALYZING & INTERPRETING ETHNOGRAPHIC DATA

MARGARET D. LeCOMPTE
JEAN J. SCHENSUL

5 ETHNOGRAPHER'S
TOOLKIT

ALTAMIRA
PRESS

A Division of Sage Publications, Inc.
Walnut Creek ◆ London ◆ New Delhi

For information:

AltaMira Press
A Division of Sage Publications, Inc.
1630 North Main Street, Suite 367
Walnut Creek, California 94596 USA
explore@altamira.sagepub.com
http://www.altamirapress.com

SAGE Publications, Ltd.
6 Bonhill Street
London, EC2A 4PU
United Kingdom

SAGE Publications India Pvt. Ltd.
M-32 Market
Greater Kailash I
New Delhi 100 048
India

Printed in the United States of America

Library of Congress Cataloging-in-Publications Data

LeCompte, Margaret Diane.
  Analyzing and interpreting ethnographic data / by Margaret D.
LeCompte and Jean J. Schensul.
    p. cm. — (Ethnographer's toolkit; v. 5)
  Includes bibliographical references and index.
  ISBN 0-7619-8974-9 (pbk.: alk. paper)
    1. Ethnology—Methodology. I. Schensul, Jean J. II. Title.
III. Series.
  GN345.L42 1999
  305.8′001—dc21   99-6243

This book is printed on acid-free paper.

99 00 01 02 03 9 8 7 6 5 4 3 2 1

Production Editor: Astrid Virding
Editorial Assistant: Nevair Kabakian
Designer/Typesetter: Janelle LeMaster
Cover Design: Ravi Balasuriya
Cover Artists: Ed Johnetta Miller, Graciela Quiñones Rodriguez

CONTENTS

LIST OF FIGURES

LIST OF TABLES

INTRODUCTION

The **Ethnographer's Toolkit** is a series of texts on how to plan, design, carry out, and use the results of applied ethnographic research. Ethnography, as an approach to research, may be unfamiliar to people accustomed to more traditional forms of research, but we believe that applied ethnography will prove not only congenial but essential to many researchers and practitioners. Many kinds of evaluative or investigative questions that arise in the course of program planning and implementation cannot really be answered very well with standard research methods such as experiments or collection of quantifiable data. Often, there are no data yet to quantify or programs whose effectiveness needs to be assessed! Sometimes, the research problem to be addressed is not yet clearly identified and must be discovered. In such cases, ethnographic research provides a valid and important way to find out what *is* happening in programs and to help practitioners plan their activities.

This book series defines what ethnographic research is; when it should be used; and how it can be used to identify and solve complex social problems, especially those not readily amenable to traditional quantitative or experimental research methods alone. It is designed for educators; service professionals; professors of applied students in the fields of teaching, social and health services, communications, engineering, and business; and students working in applied field settings.

Ethnography is a peculiarly human endeavor; many of its practitioners have commented that, unlike other approaches to research, the researcher is the primary tool for collecting primary data. That is, as Books 1, 2, 3, and 4 demonstrate, the ethnographer's principal database is amassed in the course of human interaction: direct observation; face-to-face interviewing and elicitation; audiovisual recording; and mapping the networks, times, and places in which human interactions occur. Thus, as Book 6 makes clear, the personal characteristics and activities of researchers as human beings and as scientists become salient in ways not applicable in research where the investigator can maintain more distance from the people and phenomena under study.

Book 1 of the **Ethnographer's Toolkit,** *Designing and Conducting Ethnographic Research,* places ethnography within the range of research methods in the social sciences and defines what ethnographic research is. It addresses the most important uses for ethnographic research and describes the predominant viewpoints or paradigms that guide its execution. It also provides the reader with an overview of research methods and design, including how to develop research questions, what to consider in setting up the mechanics of a research project, and how to devise a sampling plan. The book concludes with a discussion of strategies for collecting and analyzing data, and ethical consideration for which ethnographers must account in the field.

In Book 2 of the **Ethnographer's Toolkit,** *Essential Ethnographic Methods,* readers are provided with an introduction to participant and nonparticipant observation, interviewing, and ethnographically informed survey research, including systematically administered structured interviews and questionnaires. These data collection strategies are fundamental to good ethnographic research. The essential methods provide ethnographers with tools to answer the principal ethnographic questions: "What's happening in this setting?" "Who is engaging in what kind of activities?" and "Why are they doing what they are doing?" Ethnographers use them to enter a field situation and obtain basic information about social structure, social events, cultural patterns, and the meanings people give to these patterns. The essential tools also permit ethnographers to learn about new situations from the perspective of insiders because they require ethnographers to become involved in the local cultural setting and to acquire their knowledge through hands-on experience.

In Book 3, *Enhanced Ethnographic Methods*, the reader adds to this basic inventory of ethnographic tools three different but important approaches to data collection, each one a complement to the essential methods presented in Book 2. These tools are audiovisual techniques, focused group interviews, and elicitation techniques. We have termed these data collection strategies "enhanced" ethnographic methods because each of them parallels and enhances a strategy first presented in Book 2.

Audiovisual techniques, which involve recording behavior and speech using electronic equipment, expand the capacity of ethnographers to observe and listen by creating a more complete and permanent record of events and speech. Focused group interviews permit ethnographers to interview more than one person at a time. Elicitation techniques allow ethnographers to quantify qualitative or perceptual data on how individuals and groups of people think about and organize perceptions of their cultural world.

It is important for the reader to recognize that, whereas the essential ethnographic methods described in Book 2 can be used alone, the enhanced ethnographic methods covered in Book 3 cannot, by themselves, provide a fully rounded picture of cultural life in a community, organization, work group, school, or other setting. Instead, they must be used in combination with the essential methods outlined in Book 2. Doing so adds dimensions of depth and accuracy to the cultural portrait constructed by the ethnographer.

In Book 4, *Mapping Social Networks, Spatial Data, and Hidden Populations,* we add to the enhanced methods of data collection and analysis used by ethnographers. However, the approach taken in Book 4 is informed by a somewhat different perspective on the way social life is organized in communities. Whereas the previous books focus primarily on ways of understanding cultural patterns and the interactions of individuals and groups in cultural settings, Book 4 focuses on how social networks and patterns of interaction, and uses of what we term "sociogeographic space," influence human behavior and beliefs.

Book 6, *Researcher Roles and Research Partnerships,* explores the special requirements that ethnographic research imposes on its practitioners. The authors first describe how the work of the ethnographer is inextricably tied to the personal qualities of the individual research, the cultural context of the research site, and the roles and relationships that ethnographers establish. Then, they examine how ethnographers assemble research teams and collaboratively establish partnerships with individuals and institutions to solve community problems. It also discusses institutional, professional, and ethical considerations important to ethnographic research.

The last book in the series, *Using Ethnographic Data: Interventions, Public Programming, and Public Policy,* consists of three chapters that present general guidelines and case studies illustrating how ethnographers have used ethnographic data in planning public programs, developing and evaluating interventions, and influencing public policy.

The authors use rich case examples to describe ways to make ethnographic research policy relevant; how to deal with policymakers and the media; how to use ethnography to design, operate, and evaluate programs; and how ethnographic information can assist the cultural and social institutions of the community.

In this book, *Analyzing and Interpreting Ethnographic Data,* we provide the reader with a variety of methods for transforming piles of fieldnotes, observations, audio- and videotapes, questionnaires, surveys, documents, maps, and other kinds of data into research results that help people to understand their world more fully and facilitate problem solving. Addressing both narrative and qualitative, as well as quantitative—or enumerated—data, Book 5 discusses methods for organizing, retrieving, rendering manageable, and interpreting the data collected in ethnographic research. In Chapters 1 through 6, we discuss how researchers analyze qualitative data, starting with processes of inscription, description, and transcription of fieldnotes, as well as transforming documentary data and unstructured and semistructured interviews into research results. We distinguish between research results and research findings; the former are the result of analysis of data, whereas the latter derive from interpretation of previously analyzed data. We also describe how researchers clean up, organize, and code such data. Chapter 7 presents ways to organize roughly analyzed data into more abstract patterns and structures. Chapters 8 and 9 shift to a discussion of strategies for using theoretical frameworks as an aid to analyzing quantitative data and indicate how quantitative and qualitative data can, and should, be combined in a single research study. Chapter 9 presents the most commonly used statistical procedures used for quantitative analysis. Chapter 10 focuses on display of data; researchers "know" what they can "show," and showing what they have learned requires considerable ingenuity. We have provided a wide range of illustrative examples. Finally, Chapter 11 discusses the interpretation of data, helping the reader to understand how to determine, and then to present to varied audiences what the data really mean.

Throughout the series, authors give examples drawn from their own work and the work of their associates. These examples and case studies present ways in which ethnographers have coped with the kinds of problems and dilemmas found in the field—and described in the series—in the course of their work and over extended periods of time.

Readers less familiar with ethnographic research will gain an introduction to basic ethnographic principles, methods, and techniques by reading Books 1, 2, 5, and 6 first, followed by other books that explore more specialized areas of research and use. Those familiar with basic ethnographic methods will find Books 3, 4, and 7 valuable in enhancing their repertoires of research methods, data collection techniques, and ways of approaching the use of ethnographic data in policy and program settings.

—Jean J. Schensul and Margaret D. LeCompte

1

ANALYSIS AND INTERPRETATION

*Analysis
Defined*
•
*Interpretation
Defined*

Ethnographers have only three basic kinds of data: **Key point**
information about what people say, what they do,
and what they leave behind in the form of manufactured
artifacts and documents. As we have noted in Books 1, 2, 3,
and 4 of the **Ethnographer's Toolkit,** researchers have devised many ingenious ways to collect such information, all
based on observing and talking to human beings. These
methods range from very unobtrusive to very obvious, and
from very undirected to highly directed. They can involve
the very unobtrusive collection of publicly available documents and objects that people produce as they work and
interact with each other. For example, fieldworkers do unobtrusive data collection when they assemble the agendas,
minutes, proposals, and other documents that organizations pass out to their members, or when they monitor the
wear or traces left by human beings, as museum curators
do when they measure the popularity of exhibits by determining where the greatest accumulation of trash occurs and
in front of which exhibits the flooring must be replaced.
Curators reason that the more the floor wears, and the more
trash that needs to be collected, the greater the number of
people who passed by the given exhibit (Webb, Campbell,
Schwartz, & Sechrest, 1996).

1

Somewhat more obtrusive is nonparticipant observation; if participants in the research project know that they are being watched, they may alter their behavior to conform with what they think is appropriate for the researcher to see. More obtrusive methods include those that require interaction with research participants, including in-depth interviews, elicitation techniques, and ethnographic surveying. The most intimate and intrusive of strategies are the kinds of participant observation that require the researcher to follow people around, live in their neighborhoods and homes, join them in their workplaces, and generally become part of the community under study.

Regardless of the way data are collected, at some point, usually about halfway through a research project, ethnographers begin to notice that their briefcases, offices, closets, hallways, and even their cars have begun to overflow with data: stacks of interviews; piles of fieldnotes; collections of reports, documents, and newspaper clippings; boxes of audio- and videotapes; and hundreds and hundreds of cards and slips of paper. Unfortunately, by themselves, these

 Key point

materials do not create an ethnography. *Rather, ethnographers create ethnography in a sometimes tedious and often exhilarating two-step process of analysis and interpretation of those materials.* It is these processes that turn piles of data into a story worth telling.

Definition:
Analysis
reduces data
to a story that
ethnographers can
tell; interpretation
tells readers what
that story means

Analysis of data reduces them to a more manageable form that permits ethnographers to tell a story about the people or group that is the focus of their research; **interpretation** of that story permits ethnographers to describe to a reader what the story means. Often, this has to be done on at least two levels. The first level is what makes the ethnographer's story meaningful to insiders, or the people who have been studied. The second level involves making the results meaningful to—or translated for—outsiders, who can represent many different audiences or constituencies. This book will detail just how analysis and interpretation are done.

ANALYSIS DEFINED

Harry Wolcott (1988), a noted anthropologist, says that the goal of analysis is to create less data, not more. Wolcott does not really mean that ethnographers lose data when they analyze them; rather, the raw data are coded, counted, tallied, and summarized so that what the ethnographer ends up with are much more concise collections of "crunched" data (Goetz & LeCompte, 1978) rather than piles of interviews and file cabinets full of fieldnotes. Michael Patton (1987), an evaluation researcher, says that analysis does three things:

- It brings order to the piles of data an ethnographer has accumulated.
- It turns the big piles of raw data into smaller piles of crunched or summarized data.
- It permits the ethnographer to discover patterns and themes in the data and to link them with other patterns and themes.

Analysis, then, turns raw data into "cooked data" or "results." Results are descriptions of what happened in a study and are a critical step leading to the end product—interpretations and implications for more research, intervention, or action—but they are not the final step in the research project. Below are some results from a study LeCompte did of The Learning Circle, an after-school program designed to improve the academic achievement and participation in school of American Indian elementary school children.

EXAMPLE 1.1   ⬤—•—⬤—•—⬤

RESULTS FROM A STUDY OF THE LEARNING CIRCLE

After reading and rereading daily teacher schedules, transcripts of interviews conducted with teachers, fieldnotes taken while accompanying teachers on home visits, and records of parent conversations made during evening parent meetings, Learning Circle researchers confirmed their initial impression that a consistent style of interaction existed between the parents of Learning Circle children and the program staff. The researchers had noticed that (a) parents always were contacted by the certified teachers who worked with their children, rather than social workers, paraprofessionals, or other lower-status, nonacademic personnel; (b) considerable effort was made to give the parents advance notice of visits; (c) parents were provided with many choices in how they worked with the educational materials the teachers left in the homes for child and parent usage; (d) parent meetings always involved a meal or refreshments—a practice denoting a significant event in American Indian culture; and (e) parents were encouraged to provide ideas for the curriculum.

⬤—•—⬤—•—⬤

These results, in this case, patterns in the data, do not just speak for themselves. Results have to be given meaning beyond the immediate setting, put into the context of the research questions that the researcher is trying to answer, and displayed in a form that conveys their meaning to the people for whom such information is useful. LeCompte and her associates (LeCompte, Aguilera, Fordemwalt, Wilks, & Wiertelak, 1996) decided that, taken together, these activities denoted a pattern of respect for American Indian parents and their culture, and perhaps more important, that the pattern differed significantly from the way Indian parents were treated in any other school or social service agency they encountered in the city. Their interpretation was corroborated in interviews with parents, who stated repeatedly that they felt respected and as though the Learning Circle was one of the few places in white society to which they really belonged.

INTERPRETATION DEFINED

Interpretation, or going beyond results, is the goal of the second step of the analytic process. Interpreting, or giving meaning to, data involves figuring out what the crunched data mean, or what they say about the people, groups, or programs that the ethnographer has been studying. This involves attaching meaning and significance to the patterns, themes, and connections that the researcher identified during analysis; explaining why they have come to exist; and indicating what implications they might have for future actions.

Taken together, the processes of analysis and interpretation can be viewed as a series of stages in which a whole phenomenon is dissected, divided into its components, and then reassembled in terms of definitions or explanations that make the phenomenon understandable to outsiders. Elsewhere, we have called this process "playing with ideas" and likened it to putting jigsaw puzzles together.

> The edge pieces are located first and assembled to provide a frame of reference. Then attention is devoted to those more striking aspects of the puzzle picture that can be identified readily from the mass of pieces and assembled separately. Next [after sneaking a look at the puzzle picture on the box for hints,] the puzzle worker places the assembled parts in their general position within the frame, and finally locates and adds the connecting pieces until no holes remain. (LeCompte & Preissle, 1993, p. 237)

If analysis creates the chunks of data that portray what the researcher discovered, then interpretation of data permits researchers to answer some of the most important questions that researchers and nonresearchers ask. These include the following:

- Why are people acting like this?
- What's going wrong—or right—with our program?

- What else do we need to know?
- What is the best course of action for us to take?
- Is this strategy or program effective?
- What kind of program would be best for us to implement?
- What new things have we learned?
- What new insights have we gained?

In the first part of this book, we will talk about analysis and interpretation of what is commonly, if awkwardly, called "qualitative" data. Qualitative data are descriptive; they pertain to the qualities or characteristics of people, places, events, phenomena, and organizations. Qualitative data can be recorded in a manner that is relatively easy to crunch or analyze, as data collected via systematic or standardized surveys are. Or, they can be very complex renderings that address such complicated issues as the characteristics of relationships, the origin of events or problems, and the reasons why events transpire as they do.

Analyzing such data requires a rather different approach than is familiar to many researchers. As we indicated in Book 1 of the **Ethnographer's Toolkit,** many kinds of research designs relegate analysis and interpretation to the final stages of the research process; data are first collected, and when data collection is complete, analysis begins, sometimes long after the researcher has left the field or the laboratory. However, ethnographers begin analysis of qualitative data almost as soon as they enter the field site; they continue the process of analysis, hypothesis creation and testing, and interpretation throughout the process of collecting qualitative and quantitative data, until the final page of the last report is written. This occurs because ethnography usually is conducted under conditions of some uncertainty about the direction of the study, the kinds of data that will be most relevant, and even which questions are most salient to ask. Researchers may have begun with a research question, or the desire to explore the origins of a specific social problem, only to find out when they are in the field that the original problem is not a problem to research participants in the field, or that a different issue is much more important than the one with which the researcher started. Or, the researcher may have begun with a general theoretical model or way of thinking about the world, only to find that this model is not congruent with the way people in the field explain their world.

➤•➤•➤ **EXAMPLE 1.2**

COMPETING VIEWS OF CAUSALITY IN A NAVAJO SCHOOL DISTRICT

LeCompte and her associates found that there were distinct and competing explanations for why so many unfortunate events had happened in the school district they were studying. The gymnasium roof had begun to leak during a sudden rainstorm, flooding the newly installed basketball floor and ruining it. Two faculty members had developed fatal illnesses. More than one fourth of the students in high school were failing at least one subject. And morale of teachers and staff was so low that a number of the district's best teachers were planning to leave at the end of the school year. The assistant superintendent and the researchers attributed the problems to general bad luck, a building boom in the area that had made it difficult to find competent construction workers for the gym roof repairs, and an autocratic new high school principal who had alienated students and teachers alike. Teacher turnover always was high in this district, the assistant superintendent explained, because it attracted young teachers interested in Indians and Indian culture. They soon became disenchanted when they found out just how isolated the community was and that the local Navajos were not very interested in getting to know them. He suggested recruiting teachers who were less naive and more competent, and figuring out appropriate grounds to dismiss and replace the high school principal. By contrast, many of the Indian staff felt that the discord and misfortune in the district resulted from an imbalance between the forces of man, the Holy People, and nature. The disharmony had been caused by some as-yet-unknown transgression; it would be redressed if a traditional healing ceremony to restore harmony were performed on behalf of the district and its personnel (LeCompte & McLaughlin, 1994).

➤•➤•➤

This example shows major differences between a Western, scientific rationale for events and the more traditional Navajo definition of the problem and its solution. In fact, the district used both strategies to help solve its problems.

EXAMPLE 1.3 ➤•➤•➤

COMPETING EXPLANATIONS FOR THE ORIGINS
OF BLINDNESS AMONG CAMBODIAN REFUGEES

A number of refugees who managed to escape the "killing fields" of Cambodia and find their way to California had become blind, although their vision had been unimpaired in Cambodia and they reported no disease or trauma that could have damaged their eyes. Social service personnel arranged medical examinations for the refugees, only to have the doctors say that from a physiological standpoint, their eyes were not impaired. Neurological testing showed that when presented with visual stimuli, the refugees could "see"—as measured by brain waves—even though the people reported that they saw nothing. Convinced that the refugees were not lying or faking, social service personnel probed further and found that all of the people who were blind without apparent cause had witnessed the most horrific acts of savagery, including the murder and torture of their families, entire villages, and thousands of other people by the Khmer Rouge. The social workers reasoned that the refugees simply could not bear to witness any more horrors. Their brains had created some kind of psychological block that prevented visual stimuli from being recognized as sight, thus rendering them "blind." A remedy for the blindness lay not in medical treatment but in psychocultural and perhaps traditional shamanistic therapy for their posttraumatic stress.[1]

➤•➤•➤

Careful sleuthing by workers with cultural sensitivity helped find a reasonable, if unusual, explanation for the blindness of the refugees, one that modern medicine could not come up with. Ethnographers need to realize that if they are not open to new ways of formulating what they observe in the research site, they may not fully understand what they have observed during their fieldwork. The recursive analytic processes in which ethnographers engage permit them to revise original formations, raise different questions, and even come to conclusions far removed from what they originally anticipated. To that end, we discuss three stages of the analysis process:

- Analysis done while still in the field
- Analysis done as soon as the study is complete, preferably while still in the field, but certainly as soon as one returns from the field
- Analysis done after some time or at some distance from the field

NOTE

1. An excellent description of similar miscommunication and total lack of understanding between Hmong/Laotian refugees and medical personnel can be found in Anne Fadiman's *The Spirit Catches You and You Fall Down* (1997).

2 ━●━●━●━

IN-THE-FIELD ANALYSIS

As we have made clear in Books 1 through 4, ethnographers spend a lot of time asking questions of people, observing them, and writing down information about what they say and do in their home communities and workplaces. In the process, ethnographers make many decisions about what should be observed. They also continuously follow hunches—which we could call hypotheses—that help them figure out why things happen as they do. The recursive process of questioning constantly; getting answers; asking more refined questions; getting more complete answers; and looking for instances that clarify, modify, or negate the original formulations permits ethnographers to reorder their sense of what is happening. Especially important is the search for **negative evidence**, or instances, events, behavior, or other facts that appear to disconfirm what the ethnographer has already found. It is all too tempting to discard these cases as anomalies or simply as incorrect. Miles and Huberman (1984) argue that the time spent trying to figure out how negative cases inform the ethnographer's understanding is well worth it because sometimes these cases provide the strongest argument for refining or modifying the research.

Definition: Negative evidence disconfirms initial hunches or conclusions

11

EXAMPLE 2.1 ━━●━━●━━

HOW BIG IS THE SCHOOL DISTRICT? RECURSIVITY AND NEGATIVE EVIDENCE

"Pinnacle" United School District, the Navajo Nation district that LeCompte studied, had an enrollment of slightly more than 2,000 students in four schools (elementary, intermediate, middle, and high school), all located within easy walking distance of each other. Compared to the other districts with which LeCompte had worked, Pinnacle was a very tiny district that she felt should have had miminal problems with communication and supervision. Administrators, however, kept attributing their difficulty in implementing curricular reforms to the fact that the district was "so big." LeCompte puzzled long and hard over this discrepancy between the actual size of the district and the perception of its size held by the staff. Only when the superintendent explicitly compared his district to a neighboring one with fewer than 300 students did LeCompte understand that perception of size was relative. All of the Navajo districts were extremely isolated both physically and culturally from larger, off-reservation, mainstream districts. This meant that they compared themselves to each other rather than to larger districts off the reservation. The Pinnacle school district was, in fact, one of the larger districts in the Navajo Nation; its administrators were using the even tinier districts around them as a reference point. By treating the assertions of "bigness" by Pinnacle administrators as negative evidence, LeCompte was not only able to clear up a puzzling conflict in perceptions, but also to learn more about just how important a cultural factor the isolation of the district was (LeCompte & Wiertelak, 1994).

━━●━━●━━

 Key point   *Recursive analysis of the kind just described is done from the moment an ethnographer enters the field to the point at which the last page of the final report is written.* However, it is applied somewhat differently at different stages of the analytic process. The first set of procedures—inscription, description, and transcription (which we describe in the following pages)—is carried out in the field, often on the fly, on one's feet, and by the seat of one's pants. These procedures require exhausting and scrupulous attention to the details of listening and observing, as well as attention to one's own inner organizational schemes and biases. They also require hours of typing up fieldnotes and a good system for filing or cataloging data.

The second set of procedures involves "tidying up" data right after the fieldwork is completed; the final stage is what is more commonly recognized as data management and analysis: a laborious process of organizing and "cooking" raw data until they become research results. In the next section, we describe the analytic processes that ethnographers use in the initial stages of qualitative fieldwork: inscription, description, and transcription (Clifford, 1990).

INSCRIPTION

Inscription is the act of making mental notes prior to writing things down. Such mental notes might be made during a pause in conversation or a break in activities, as an ethnographer mentally "refers to some prior list of questions, traits or hypotheses" (Clifford, 1990, p. 51) and then jots down a mnemonic word or phrase to help in remembering what he or she wants to investigate. This may seem simple enough, but in the initial stages of an ethnographic study, all ethnographers have a difficult time figuring out *what* to write down, or what to write about. Many advisors to novice ethnographers urge them to take care to record everything—advice that has led to extreme frustration among many new fieldworkers, who find it impossible. In the first place, although field sites vary in their degree of confusion and complexity, they are always a whirling, buzzing maelstrom of activity. Does one look at the physical environment? the people? which specific people? or all of them? and what if they are doing many different things? Imagine a carnival, a large outdoor market, a clinic waiting room, or a crowded school classroom. Where would one start?

Cross Reference: See Book 2, Chapter 4, on observing and recording data when entering the field

In addition to the impossibility of recording everything at once when "everything" is happening at the same time, ethnographers often face the difficult task of trying to register what is actually happening in a totally unfamiliar setting. Sometimes, they have difficulty even finding a vocabulary to describe events and objects that they have never seen before and with which they have had no prior experience (see Clifford, 1990). Making the task manageable requires some form of selective attention and translation.

All people, including all ethnographers, tend to notice first—and to write down—what they have already learned to notice. We have been trained—consciously and unconsciously—to attend to those items, domains, events, objects, animals, plants, people, and behaviors in our environment that our culture defines as worthy of notice and helpful to our survival. One of the first lessons that ethnographers must learn is how to get outside of their own heads, or how to go beyond their own ethnocentric frameworks for valuing, noticing, and naming so that they can begin to notice—and to write down information about—items, domains, events, objects, animals, plants, people, and behaviors that have been defined as noteworthy to other, often quite different, people and cultures.

 Cross Reference: See Book 1, Chapter 1, for defining characteristics of ethnography

Key point

Thus, the process of inscription involves learning to notice what is important to other people and what one has not been trained to see, and then to write it down. However, writing it down inevitably is done, at least to some degree, through the lens of the ethnographer, who inscribes them from his or her own frame of reference. Even to notice something is to have some prior idea that it is worth noticing; part of the ethnographic endeavor is first learning what is worth noticing to others, and then describing it in a way that makes sense to those others as well. Thus, although the initial stages of writing things down does, in fact, involve creating a mental text, they also involve recreating or modifying a text or set of ideas about that subject that already exists in the mind of the ethnographer. The creation of an initial conceptual or operational model early in the research process is very helpful in focusing questions, observations, social and geographic mapping operations, and the recording of event sequences. Interviews with key informants in the first stages of an ethnographic study also help to frame the exploration process through the eyes of the participants.

Much of the mental text of the ethnographer is a consequence of his or her past personal experiences and characteristics. However, what researchers attend to in the field and, hence, what they inscribe also is very much influenced by the research questions they have asked or how the researcher has been trained to think about and conceptualize the world. For example, early anthropologists were trained in functional theory, which stated that the purpose of any human society was to carry out basic functions necessary for that society to survive. These include reproduction (carried out by kinship systems and families, or sometimes by recruitment of new members); transmission of culture (carried out by families, schools, churches, and other socializing institutions); distribution of resources (carried out in markets, manufacturing agencies, trade organizations, and systems of exchange); aesthetics (exemplified in the practice of the arts, handicrafts, and creative activities); and many other functions. Early fieldwork—and the process of inscription—focused on identifying and describing how these various functions were carried out. Contemporary ethnographers, by contrast, focus less often on creating theoretically informed descriptions of a whole society than they do on using theories about specific human processes to identify and explain smaller chunks or aspects of societies. In the following example, we describe how theories about human learning and formation of gender identity helped to structure the inscription process in a study of an educational innovation. We also demonstrate how ethnographers must take care not to miss important elements of

Cross Reference:
See Book 2, Chapters 2 and 3, for a systematic discussion of how to formulate an initial working model

Key point

Cross Reference:
See Book 6 for a discussion of how researcher characteristics and experiences affect what they do and can observe in the field

the culture under study because they simply do not think they are important.

EXAMPLE 2.2 ━━●━━●━●━━

INSCRIBING INFORMATION ON ARTS INSTRUCTION IN THE ARTS FOCUS STUDY

Even before they began their study of an arts program at Centerline Middle School, LeCompte and Holloway were puzzling over the potential impact that education in the arts might have on the cognitive growth, self-confidence, and identity development of young adolescents.

Based on her readings of the sociocultural learning theorist Lev Vygotsky (1934, 1978), LeCompte wondered about the degree to which specific strategies in arts instruction could foster higher-level thinking skills such as evaluation, hypothesis testing, and intellectual risk taking. Although LeCompte had had some music training, and Holloway was a writer who had taught creative writing, neither researcher had had much experience in visual or performing arts—the two strongest strands in the program.

Having read the work of the developmental psychologist Carol Gilligan (Gilligan, 1982; Gilligan, Lyons, & Hanmer, 1990; Gilligan, Taylor, & Sullivan, 1995) and others, Holloway was particularly interested in whether or not arts education would help young women develop less traditional career goals. LeCompte tended to pay particular attention, then, to instructional activities that required students to engage in critique or to "think about unthinkable things," imagine events or activities to be different from what they were or the way they had always been done, or try on new ideas. Holloway watched closely for differences between the reactions of boys and girls and for instances when girls took on activities usually reserved for boys. The two researchers tended to watch for these kinds of things during regular classroom instruction because they deemed these activities to be most important. However, the calisthenics, games, and noise making in which the theater class systematically engaged at the beginning of each class period did not look very much like instruction to the researchers, except perhaps as a way to help lively 11- to 15-year-old children blow off steam and settle down before "real" instruction began.

Even though they wrote down everything and had, in fact, made detailed notes on the vigorous pretheater activities, the researchers found that their early fieldnotes were filled with references to ways of thinking and differences between boys and girls as they existed in regular instruction—the original focus of the study and what the researchers thought to be most important. It was not until they began to interview theater students, and found that students viewed the "warm-ups" done at the beginning of the day to be among the most valuable things they learned, that the researchers looked more closely at these calisthenics, games, and vocal exercises—to which they had not paid much attention previously. The warm-ups were, in fact, activities that transformed the school experience for students. They helped students relax, reduce stress, and focus their concentration; most important to the study, the students argued that they were useful in their other, nonart classes.

━•━•━

LeCompte and Holloway first inscribed data that were congruent with their initial interests; however, they also tried to make careful note of things that did not make sense to them. In this way, they learned to attend to things that, although they were not originally defined as important to researchers, turned out to be very important for the people in the study. As LeCompte and Holloway learned, how you inscribe depends on how you conceive of the study and how you want to tell its story.

DESCRIPTION

Description occurs after inscription. Description involves writing things down in jottings, diaries, logs, and fieldnotes (Bernard, 1995, p. 181) and producing "thick descriptions" (Geertz, 1973), or narratives of events, behaviors, conversations, activities, interpretations, and explanations that, taken together, help to create a portrayal of the soul and heart of a group, community, organization, or culture. Descriptions are the "more or less coherent representations of an observed cultural reality" (Clifford, 1990, p. 51). In creating them, ethnographers stop the clock; that is, they hold present time constant while they reorder the recent past that they have observed and jotted down. Then, they systematize it, put it in context with prior events about which they have learned in the course of the fieldwork, and turn it into evidence to be assembled into the database from which the full ethnographic account will be created (Clifford, 1990, pp. 51-52).

Fieldnotes are produced in a quiet place away from the site of observation and interaction with people in the field. They include reflection, preliminary analyses, initial interpretations, and new questions and hunches to be answered and tested in the next days and weeks of observation. *Fieldnotes, as we shall see, are organized around those basic conceptual frames or questions that structured the study in the first place; they become increasingly focused and "precoded" as the research itself progresses and homes in on those features of the cultural scene that become most interesting and as the formative theoretical model emerges.* Semistructured data collection (structured, open-ended interviews and specifically targeted and timed observations) on selected topics related to the study helps to identify and affirm preliminary hunches and associations that can later be confirmed statistically using structured survey methods.

 Key point

TRANSCRIPTION

Transcription also creates fieldnotes. It is a rather more formal process than is recording of naturalistic observations, and it occurs throughout the fieldwork stages of a research process. It often continues into the early stages of analysis away from the field. Transcription is sometimes thought to be only the word-for-word creation of a written text from an audio- or videotaped account given by an informant. However, Clifford (1990) defines the term much more broadly to include any kind of elicitation from an informant, whether it be

Cross Reference: See Books 1 and 2 for methods of eliciting information via interviews, and Book 3 for methods using audio and visual recording, focus groups, and formalized elicitation techniques

- Writing down the *verbatim* responses of informants to interviews
- Taking dictation
- Recording stories, legends, spells, ditties, chants, or songs
- Keeping a running record of everything an individual says during a specific period of observation

We would add to this list respondents' commentaries when engaged in listing and sorting exercises, a mapping of the location of events and activities, sentence completions, responses to photographs and other visual stimulation, and responses to surveying.

Focusing as it does on spoken language, transcription is particularly important for linguistic studies when the objective of the research is collection of indigenous texts and stories or gaining an understanding of the meanings attributed to specific behaviors.

Nonverbal behavior, however, also can be a focus of transcription. For example, school personnel often script the behavior of teachers whom they want to evaluate; this involves keeping a detailed written record of what the teacher says and does during a given period of monitoring. Similar scripting often is done in detailed monitoring of human behavior in situations where videotaping is not possible or is inappropriate, such as in classrooms.

Transcription, then, involves writing down verbatim, photographing, videotaping, or "copying," in Clifford's terms, what an informant says he or she knows of a tradition, practice, event, custom, ritual, myth, or song. Or, in the case of scripting, it is a detailed record of what a single person is observed to say and do in a given situation. Below are several examples of transcripts. One of the sources of data for the study of Arts Focus was a set of more than 100 audiotapes of interviews that the researchers had conducted with students, teachers, and administrators in the program. These audiotapes had to be transcribed mechanically and looked like the following example.

EXAMPLE 2.3   ➤•➤•➤

TRANSCRIPT FROM AN INTERVIEW WITH A SIXTH-GRADE MALE ARTS FOCUS STUDENT, AGED ABOUT 11

DH: Hi. As I told you, my name is Deb, and we are working on an evaluation of the Arts Focus program. I know I've seen you in class this year, JT; I'm really happy that you agreed to talk with us because I think it's really important that we find out what students think about the program. So first, I want to ask you a few background questions. Why did you choose to be in the literary arts program?

JT: I don't know. Well, I really thought I was good at, well, writing, and I thought it was fun, so my plan was that I'd do the literary arts because I'd really enjoy that. Then I wanted to go to visual arts [next year] because I really like drawing, you know, things like that.

DH: So when you say you really like literary arts, what is it about literary arts?

JT: Well, it's the freedom we have. I don't know, it's so concentrated and it's like, you are just surrounded by writers and books . . .

DH: Before you came to the program, did you write a lot?

JT: Yes. Not as much creatively, but you know, in science. I don't know, it was more the case of a journal than actually writing. I decided that I enjoyed writing and also I enjoy being creative.

DH: So you just did it!

JT: Yeah.

DH: Have you taken classes in any other arts areas, other than writing?

JT: Well, when I was little, I took art classes, I think I took something in the art museum.

DH: So you did visual-oriented art?

JT: Yeah.

DH: OK.

JT: See, I'm not into, well, I think I'd be good at drama, and I think it's fun to act out, and we kind of, I think it's easier not to be yourself, actually. Because a whole bunch of people would know that you are not purposely being an idiot. Yes, but, like singing, no, that's not for me. The drawing, yes. I probably draw every other day or something.

DH: You do? Right now?

JT: Yes. Or maybe more, unless I have too much homework. Or at least I pay attention more on my homework . . .

DH: Than you did before?

JT: Yeah.

DH: Let me ask you a few questions about your literary arts class. Can you tell me what you do in your literary arts class?

JT: There's this five minute . . . sort of like where I don't get focused, then I'll make sure nobody's looking and I'll run to the other side of the room [Note: the class meets in the school's very large library] where we have a little place. I just write until we [the teacher and he] have our meeting, or whatever. There's not many distractions, but I'm an easily distracted person, so I have to find a good spot.

━●━●━

The following are excerpts from an ethnographic interview conducted by Lorie Broomhall, an anthropologist at the Institute for Community Research involved in ethnographic research with young drug users (Broomhall, Wilson, & Singer, 1998).

EXAMPLE 2.4 ━•━•━

TRANSCRIBING IN-DEPTH INTERVIEWS WITH YOUNG DRUG USERS

L: What name do you want me to use for you in this interview?

D: Danny.

L: Danny, OK. And that's how you'll be identified so that anytime if your name accidently comes up while we're talking, we'll just switch it to Danny, OK? All right, the first thing I'm gonna ask you is to kind of tell me, um, the story of your life, you know, where you were born, your family, that stuff.

D: When I was born. . .

L: Where were you born?

D: Hartford.

L: So you grew up in Hartford?

D: Yeah, I grew up in Hartford, in the project called Charter Oak.

L: OK, the one that they're tearing down over here?

D: No, on the other side.

L: Oh, OK.

D: Well my, when I was born, a month before my uncle died, he was supposed to be my godfather. He was supposed to be my godfather. My family always talked to me about him, he never saw [me] but I always wanted to see him.

L: What was special about him?

D: I don't know, my family always talks to me about him that he loved my mother. My mother was his best sister and all that stuff.

L: How did he die?

D: Um, cancer, they told me it was cancer . . .

L: Oh, what a shame, I'm sorry.

D: And that's when most of my, two of my uncles died using drugs.

L: What were they using?

D: Heroin.

L: And how old were you? This is right around the time you were born?

D: Yeah.

L: OK.

D: About the time I was born. My uncles used to sell drugs and all that. My uncle, he's in jail right now, he started, then both my uncles, one of them came out, he's on the *** now. They been using drugs, 17, 18, 19 years ago. 20 years. So . . .

L: What's your uncle, what did he go into jail for?

D: Um, changing checks, stolen checks.

L: Both of them did, or the one that's in prison right now?

D: The other one. The one that's in prison now is for changing checks and the other one he was there for robbery, for their drug use.

L: What about your parents?

D: My parents, my father, he's an alcoholic, he's dying. My mother, she's an ex-heroin addict. She's been clean for, like, 6 years now.

L: So, she's . . . was addicted when you were born?

D: No, not when I was born, she didn't even know about drugs when I was born.

L: Oh, OK. So you were born in Hartford in Charter Oak, and are you the oldest or the youngest?

D: Yeah, I'm the oldest.

L: Of how many?

D: Of two. But I have more brothers and sisters on my father's side, but it's just me and my little brother on my mother's side.

L: How many brothers and sisters all together do you have, including half-brothers and -sisters?

D: It's like three brothers and a sister.

L: Do you see them very often?

D: Um, just my little brother by my mother's side. I see him all the time, every day, but my father's side, I do not hardly see them.

L: OK, all right, so what was it like growing up as a kid?

D: It was fun, tell you the truth, 'cause I was very spoiled.

L: Yeah?

D: Yeah, I was a spoiled little kid. I was, I usually stay over my grandmother, my grandfather, yeah, 'cause since my uncle died and stuff and he wanted to be my godfather so my grandmother and my grandfather always kept me 'cause I reminded them of him. So I, my grandmother and my grandfather, I called them mom and dad, they raised me, you know, and pretty much he bought me anything I wanted.

L: Now did they live in Charter Oak too?

D: Yeah.

L: Oh, OK.

⬤—•—⬤—•—⬤

Another form of transcription also was used in the Arts Focus study. Because audiotaping was considered to be too intrusive, the researchers took down verbatim records of the conversations in faculty, parent, and administrative meetings. These were maintained in several dozen stenographers' notebooks.[1] They were, in most cases, nearly as complete as audiotaped transcriptions and served the same purposes.

EXAMPLE 2.5 ━━●━━●━━

TRANSCRIPT FOR APRIL 2, 1997, 3:05 PM: LARGE GROUP FOR ARTS FOCUS

The meeting is in the school library conference room. Present are LeCompte and Holloway (the two researchers); the four Arts Focus teachers; two parents; and Rita, a consultant from the local arts alliance who came to help the teachers identify possible sources of grant funding for the program. Some problems quickly surface with the effectiveness of the current fund-raiser. (That individual, Sue, is not a staff member at the school but wrote the initial grant for the program, and her salary is paid from it. She is supposed to provide liaison with other arts organizations in the community.)

The teachers are talking among themselves with some dismay about how, although Sue is claiming responsibility for all grant writing, she is causing delays and problems because she will not consult with the teachers about funding proposals she is writing, and they do not know what obligations Sue's proposals might create for them if the proposals are funded. Maurita says, "She does not know what the red flags are, like that art exhibit at the university which she wanted us to attend with the kids, and there were big paintings of nudes in it. Can you imagine what the kids would have done if we'd just walked in there? We can handle that—we can preview the show and plan how to prepare the kids for it—but if we do not know what we are getting into, we'll have the whole community mad at us."

Pat (the art teacher) says, "Sue is just going off on her own, writing grants and working through Jeannette Farmer (the curriculum director with the school district). Jeannette and Fran (the Centerline principal) are in contact weekly with e-mail, and they pass materials on to Sue, but nobody is talking to us, and we are the ones who will have to implement whatever they get money for. And it might not fit in with our program."

Rita says, "What I hear from Sue is, she tells me that the teachers are not coming to see her. And I'm giving Fran professional advice about what makes grant proposals stronger—I've been telling her that you won't get funded if there isn't collaboration between the teachers and all of the people involved."

Pat notes, "We did make a wish list of all the programs we wanted to try, and John (the music teacher) was going to type it up and give it to Fran so she would know what we were interested in getting funds for." [It is clear from Rita's response that she never saw the list, and that Fran had not received it from John, either.]

Rita says, "It'd really be good if you teachers could get your curriculum planned for the next year so we'd know how to plan for extra programs. And there are a lot of opportunities." She describes the local community art show, the Arts Festival at the local museum and library, and also the school's own Arts Festival. "I have the procedures for applying for funds from the school district. Fran says there is no way to get around the school district procedures, since there are particular officials who have to sign off on all grants. This means that Sue is working on grants [she names two] right now, and she isn't collaborating with you . . . that's not the wisest course for you."

Pat (sounding frustrated) chimes in, "See, basically, this [she points at a grant proposal that Sue put in the Arts Focus teachers' mailboxes this morning] is out there, and we just didn't participate in it. Even though I totally agree with the concept [upon which the proposal is based]. I just wish that we could get help from Sue for working with arts organizations other than the [local] symphony. It just seems to me that Sue is using this program to pay her salary and make opportunities for the [local] musicians."

Rita then comments, "This is a problem. To have a successful grant, it [the proposal] needs clarity, it needs to speak directly to the questions asked. It has to be sexy, vivid, have color, catch attention. These [Sue's] proposals do not have it. I would guess that Sue is not getting all her in-kind contributions recorded correctly, either, because she does not know enough about the school and what you teachers do. You'll also need letters for support for the [local arts alliance] Council grant."

Pat asks, "Do you know about the Young Audiences Program?"

"It's from the state council for the arts," says Rita. "You have to have part of the money to hire an artist, and then they pay some of the rest of the artists' fee."

They all talk about several other grant programs and what they each might do to write their own grant proposals. They ask Rita how they could start receiving the information and newsletters on grant opportunities that previously have been going to Sue, who does not pass them on to the teachers. Then, they discuss all of the logistics needed to bring an artist to the school under the Young Audiences program—facilities, time, and administrative issues.

Deb [the research assistant] gives a report on the work of the videographer whom the research team wants to hire to film the final production of "Romeo and Juliet"; the school cannot find a professional videographer whom they could afford, but they really want to document the performance for the historical record. The husband of one of Deb's friends (who is also LeCompte's student) is a videographer, and he has volunteered to do the work. Deb says, "He usually charges $100 an hour, but he'll make a deal for us; he really likes kids' theater. He'll do the whole job for $500-$700, including the editing, and he'll also document the Arts Festival."

Maurita says, "Let's do it."

Rita says that they could get some publicity with the video on the public access television channel: "You could train your students to film your productions, and then get them on TV." There is general agreement that this would be a good idea. It is now 4:00 p.m., and I have to leave the meeting.

━━●━━●━━

The researchers also scripted the behavior of teachers during instruction so as to record nuances of their instructional style and teaching content.

TRANSCRIPT FROM LECOMPTE'S FIELDNOTES, OCTOBER 4, 1996; 1:10 P.M.,
THIRD BLOCK, THEATER ARTS CLASS, SIXTH AND SEVENTH GRADERS (AGES 11-14)

Theater Arts meets in the auditorium; it is their regular classroom. The students have been planning for their annual Halloween Night theatrical production; they will perform Ray Bradbury's "The Halloween Tree," a fantasy thriller. Maurita, the teacher, told me that she liked the play, but she also chose it because there were lots of parts in it that she could assign to girls; she says that girls can play male roles in some plays, which was good, since most theater programs have too many girls, and most plays do not have very many roles for girls. I sit in front row of the auditorium seats; the teacher is at her desk in the stage-left corner below the stage. The buzzer sounds. Two boys LEAP into the still-empty auditorium, announcing in loud theatrical voices: "I am HERE!!" They leap onto the stage. One announces, "You gotta wonder about a boy who talks like a girl . . ." He then notices a girl who just entered the room and who is nearly in tears. He runs to the back of the auditorium, puts his arm around her, and asks: "What's the matter? Are you upset?" She shrugs him off, turns away, and sits down in the back. He races back to the stage and leaps back on it. Four boys are now on stage, talking in loud voices and making theatrical gestures. They have been reading Shakespeare's "Romeo and Juliet," and they are practicing the lines. Maurita Douglas, the teacher, moves to sit on a stool on the floor just below the stage at stage center. The students enter and sit down in a tight semicircle around her. Most of the 25 students are girls—I only count five boys. There is a deaf girl with a sign language interpreter in the class; the interpreter sits just behind the teacher, signing what Maurita says to the deaf girl. Maurita begins to list the decisions they have to make today to get ready for their performance. She says: "This is a production day; we are not going to do much stage stuff today. And it is not a democracy. We can all help and take part, it is not a dictatorship, but we have to get organized. Now, I am going to need lots of volunteers—I need someone to take notes here . . ." Lots of students raise their hands to volunteer to take notes. "No, I am going to use my Assistant Director (AD) here, that's what we use Assistant Directors for." [Note: The assistant director was Danielle, the girl who was upset.] The AD jumps up to the stage, where a blackboard is located, and starts writing down the high points of the discussion. They first discuss just how many performances they should have. The AD does ballet moves on the stage behind Maurita (whose back is to her). Most of the students want to have only two performances so that they can get bigger audiences; they fear that if they have more than two, the audience on each evening will be diluted. Maurita argues for more, so that more children will have a chance to participate and they will have a longer performance experience. They hold a vote, which is 8-13 in favor of having four performances.

Maurita says, "Now, if you have other activities that conflict with performing on these nights—or on any night of a performance—that's OK; if I know right now, there are enough people in the class to make substitutes and we can still put on a production. Now, let's decide on the dates. We can't have just one performance on the second week; we'll all forget our lines. And we can't have one on Tuesday, which is a school holiday." The students all start talking at once with suggestions.

Maurita listens, and then says, "OK, we're going to vote in one minute." The AD writes the possible dates on the blackboard, and they end up deciding to have two performances on the Thursday and Friday before Halloween (which is always the 31st of October), one on the night before Halloween, and one early in the evening on Halloween night.

Maurita then changes the topic. "Now we have to talk about the stage combat. The two expert instructors are coming to tomorrow's class. You are going to practice falls, drops, body slams. You'll need something to use for a quarterstaff [a medieval weapon]. You can use an old broom handle, so bring one in, but remember to sand it with sandpaper so that there won't be any splinters in them—or you'll have splinters in your hands. Come dressed for gymnastics—old clothes—tennis shoes or gym shoes. Bring water. You'll get hot. And go to the bathroom before class. The two instructors are not going to want people wandering out to go to the bathroom." Another change in topic.

"Now, let's talk about the rehearsal schedule for the play. I know this all is boring, but we have to do this or it'll be utter chaos." Various students tell her about schedule conflicts they have: soccer practice, ballet lessons, baby-sitting, a doctor's appointment. These kids have really busy schedules with many after-school commitments. It is hard to schedule rehearsals in which all the lead actors are present. She takes notes, asking each which role they have in the play and appointing a substitute. All of the girls are still sitting in the circle around Maurita, except for Danielle, the AD, still on the stage. Four of the five boys have moved to the center of the auditorium to join Mike, an 8th-grader who is directing all the sound and light work for the play, and who just came in to inspect the light booth. Two girls get up and climb onto the stage, and begin mimicking the ballet moves that Danielle continues to make.

Maurita says, "OK, now. We have to break up into groups to talk about sound effects. You are going to have to create the sound effects that will make this play live. Get out your scripts, and move into your groups." Somewhat slowly, the students move to five places in the room—two groups in the back corners, one on stage, and two on the floor in front of the stage. Maurita tells them to read each page of the first act and think about all the sounds that might go with what's happening in the play. "It's fall, it's sort of cold; the wind is blowing and the leaves are falling. It's almost night. When you go up to the old house, what does it smell like? Imagine what you might hear. You're walking down the street, with your friends. Just brainstorm together." The kids begin to brainstorm, and it gets pretty loud. Maurita then interrupts them. "I need your attention now. I have an article I want you to use for reference. It's all about how to make sound effects. It's from a professional magazine, but you are old enough to read and understand it. It'll tell you how to make the sound of rain, thunder, horses walking down the street, squeaky doors—all kinds of things— and then tape-record them so you can have a soundtrack for the play. Now read it, and keep working, because that's what we'll have to do." Maurita does some paper-work at her desk—far stage left—and then moves around the room, listening to the discussions. The students continue their discussion until the buzzer sounds for the end of class at 2:40 p.m.

━•◆•◆•━

The example above tried to include both teacher and student activities—a somewhat daunting process in a very large room with 28 people—many of whom were engaging in different, and sometimes unrelated, activities. Somewhat different is the excerpt from the Learning to Work study, which has been coded for later analysis.

EXAMPLE 2.7

TRANSCRIPT FROM "LEARNING TO WORK" FIELDNOTES

Two Elementary Schools: A Fieldnote Excerpt

Valley School

Pat, the teacher, is sitting on a student's desk at the front of the room. The students' desks are haphazardly scattered throughout the room; four girls have pushed theirs together in a row diagonally across the room; some are clustered in twos and others are by themselves. There is no teacher desk immediately visible: It is obscured in the corner behind boxes of materials and a motorcycle engine.

9:06	Discussion	T2A	(T2A) "OK, now let's start." (Todd comes up and gives her a nickel.) "OK, now here's our new word for the day. What is it?" (She writes it on the board.) "Bazaar." (She writes *bizarre* and *bazaar* on the board, explains the differences. Goes through sentences using *bizarre* to illustrate bizarre things [italics added].)
9:10	Explication	T2A	(T2A) "OK, I would like you to pay attention. We've had some problems with money. What's a dollar sign?" (Children shout the answer. She explains how to read numbers as money.) "Now, I want you to pretend you just bought a house. Now, you gotta be careful because houses cost lots of money." Writes $2856000 on the board. Larry volunteers the decimal placement.) "Darn, I could not fool you. Let's see if I can fool this young man." (Does another. He gets it right.) "Who wants a more expensive house—Bernie?" (Does another.) "Let's see, I have not heard from some of these girls. Anna, that's what I spent at the grocery store." (Does another.)
9:15-9:30		RIA	"Decimal points are very important when we are writing numbers." (She demonstrates how to add with decimals by using money numbers. She adds them wrong so that the children can correct them, calling out corrections from the classroom.) "One way to help yourself, people, is to make sure all your dots line up. (RIA) All right, boys and girls, when you get your answers, be sure to put decimal points in."
	Getting Organized	T2A	(T2A) "OK, everybody, a pencil and a paper. We're going to do some problems." (Comes over to me and tells me that it is not what she had planned to do but that it was a good introduction to decimals and that they needed the practice in this.)
9:26-9:30		A6 T3C T2A W1B	(A6) "Remember two things. It's very important if you want a hundred—dollar signs and decimal points. (T3C) I'll give you 15 minutes to do these. (T2A) OK, are we ready to start? (W1B) When we finish this, work on contracts—your math contracts. If you do not have one, we'll have a conference and make one up for you. OK, here we go. . ."

It is important to remember that both written and audio- or videotaped transcription always involves conscious or unconscious selection and **translation.** In the Arts Focus program, researchers tended to select for recording those events, stories, and materials that seemed to be most salient to their research questions or the ideas about learning and gender that interested them. LeCompte's "Learning to Work" scripts of teacher behavior (see Example 2.7 above) placed special emphasis on noninstructional speech and behavior because her interest was in the so-called hidden curriculum (Friedenberg, 1970; Jackson, 1968) of classroom structure and organization rather than on what was learned in formal content instruction. *Thus, whatever the informants say and do, items from their speech and behavior still are selected for recording and then recorded with the researcher's purpose in mind, and with an eye toward their utility in constructing an overall argument for the study— even when the researcher is taking verbatim notes or is using a recording device.* The ethnographer's observations and subsequent descriptions and transcriptions are filtered through his or her personal, professional, cultural, and theoretical lenses as well, and therefore serve whatever agendas the researcher might have.

Definition:
Translation is the process by which the ethnographer describes in his or her own words and concepts the ideas, behaviors, and words of the people observed in the study

Key point

SUMMARY

Inscription, description, and transcription create much of the database with which an ethnographer works. A helpful way to think about these processes is to consider how Roger Sanjek (1990), an urban anthropologist, classifies fieldnotes. Sanjek suggests that there are three kinds of notes: head notes, scratch notes, and fieldnotes. Head notes are the product of inscription; they can be thought of as memories or mental notes kept in the ethnographer's head or memory until such time as it is possible to actually write things down.

The simple act of storing ideas, observations, and impressions *in one's head* causes them to be organized and retrieved according to whatever culturally determined organizational scheme the ethnographer's brain customarily uses for storage and retrieval of information. This is why we have emphasized throughout this book the need for all researchers—but especially for ethnographers—to be aware of their own ethnocentrisms and the kinds of preconceptions and unconscious biases they bring to the field "with their body" (Metz, 1978) in the form of their age, gender, ethnicity, physical size, social class, religious and cultural background, educational level, and personal style. Such awareness helps to reduce the degree to which impressions written down suffer from being filtered through the mind of the ethnographer.

Some ethnographers write down little and rely mostly on their head notes; we—and most other methodologists—regard this as a poor field technique that often leads to bad research.[2] Memory is faulty; it is subject to constant revision as subsequent events modify initial impressions; it is important to record each impression as soon as possible after it occurs to avoid erosion, modification, and even falsification of the mental record.

Sanjek's category of scratch notes consists of jottings and scribblings taken during events, in the field, or immediately after events if taking notes in the presence of research participants is inappropriate. Written on envelopes, file cards, small notebooks, or slips of paper, they are the mnemonics—often in shorthand or codes—that assist one in remembering complete head notes, they are turned into description, or real fieldnotes, as soon as the ethnographer finds the time and privacy to write everything down. Many ethnographers have written about the urgency of turning scratch notes into descriptive fieldnotes before they get "cold"—and before the remembered detail in head notes is lost in the onslaught of another day's recollection. Head notes and scratch notes are turned into descriptions, which, in turn, become fieldnotes.

Full fieldnotes are like photographs; they have a "you are there" quality (Clifford, 1990, p. 61) that makes a custom, belief, or practice perhaps visible, and at least comprehensible, not only to the ethnographer but also to outsiders. As such, they go beyond both inscription and transcription—which some methodologists call "mere description," or the close-to-the-ground recording of what one sees and hears with as little interpretation added as possible. *Going beyond description means that the fieldnotes have been written, rewritten, and written over so that they have ceased to be entirely raw data and are already at least partly cooked—at least to the extent that all of the blanks have been filled in. Full fieldnotes, then, are kept as close to raw as possible, while still capturing clearly the situation within the photographic frame in all its detail at that particular point in time.*

Key point

We stress in this chapter the recursive and sometimes even unconscious analysis that ethnographers do in the field because these early analytic processes often are not recognized as such by researchers who customarily think of analysis as occurring only once the researcher leaves the field. Although we disagree with Miles and Huberman (1984), who argue that researchers should always code their fieldnotes the same night as they are recorded,[3] we do believe that some form of holistic or implicit coding and categorizing goes on throughout the fieldwork stages of research and sets the stage for hard-nosed analysis when fieldwork is over. If researchers follow the steps described in Book 2, beginning with conceptual taxonomies that guide the investigation, this broad coding system is partially developed even prior to the study and then refined during the first stages of the study and continuously thereafter. Table 2.1 displays graphically just how we will use strategies for coding, developing taxonomies, and identifying structures and patterns within a cultural scene. This scheme is

TABLE 2.1 Linking Theoretical and Operational Levels in Ethnographic Research

	Structure	*Pattern*	*Unit*	*Item or Fact*
Domain	Family dynamics; and relationship to life achievement			
Factor		Parental discipline; and job performance		
Subfactor			Modes of parental punishment; and ability to supervise employees	
Variable				Frequency of spanking, and frequency of evaluative feedback to employees

used throughout this book and in Book 2 of the **Ethnographer's Toolkit**. These strategies help to clarify how early stages of data analysis—which we discuss in Chapters 3, 4, and 5 of this book—are linked to later stages of data analysis and interpretation.

NOTES

1. LeCompte's preference for recording field observations, given that they contain many pages, are sturdily bound spiral stenographer's pads that have a stiff cardboard back, ideal for situations lacking a table or desk upon which to write. An indicator of the indestructibility of these steno pads was the survival of one—completely filled and therefore invaluable—after LeCompte inadvertently left it on the top of her car and drove off. By the time she noticed its absence, it had lain in the middle of a busy street for 30 minutes and was run over by innumerable cars and trucks. Although its binding was crushed and two pages were rendered illegible by dirt, the rest remained intact.

2. Sanjek (1990) cites some cases where experienced researchers have had to rely almost exclusively on head notes because all of their other data were destroyed. We believe that these are exceptional cases and should not be taken as guides for novice researchers.

3. Miles and Huberman (1984) assume that researchers already have done a considerable amount of fieldwork and have developed protocols or categories of behavior, speech, and events for which they want to look before they even arrive in the field. Most ethnography today begins with a guiding theoretical framework that lends itself at least to broad-based categorization of the kind we describe in Vadeboncoeur's (1997) work, later in this book. In these cases, the coding system used constantly evolves, based on the interaction of the researcher with the field setting and the data collected to date.

3 ━━•━━•━━

TIDYING UP

The second stage of analysis involves some serious housekeeping and occurs as soon as the ethnographer has left the field. Various methodologists have called this process "data cleaning," "data management," and "cataloging." We prefer the term invented by a former graduate student, who agonized over the possibility that he had wasted 3 months doing what he called "tidying up" his data, organizing them in files, labeling the files, putting them in boxes, indexing the boxes, and then stacking them on shelves in his office where they could be retrieved easily (Romagnano, 1991). He was much relieved to learn that tidying up is a necessary and preliminary kind of analysis, one that he needed to do before he could even begin to approach a more in-depth examination of his voluminous data. Romagnano's process of tidying up was no mere paper-shuffling exercise; it was quite systematic. In this chapter, we review what tidying up involves.

STEPS IN TIDYING UP

Make Copies of All Important Materials

To the extent possible, make copies of all text materials, including transcripts, fieldnotes, surveys, interviews, questionnaires, documents, and written artifacts (Patton, 1987, p. 146).

Put All Fieldnotes in Some Sort of Order

There are many ways to put fieldnotes in order; most people keep several kinds of files. Keeping multiple kinds of files facilitates retrieval. It requires that the researcher have some idea of how he or she wants to chunk up the data, and that copies be made of everything.

Types of Files

- Chronological files, with all materials generated on any given day kept together
- Genre files, which maintain specific kinds of data—logs, maps, photographs, diaries, artifacts, story transcripts, descriptive notes, journals, meeting minutes—separately
- Cast-of-character files, which maintain separate files for everything said, done, or relevant to each significant person, group of people, or program in a study
- Event or activity files, which maintain separate files for key events and activities or categories of events and activities
- Topical files, which maintain data by a category of disease, type of meeting, specific class, theme, type of behavior, or any other topic of interest to the researcher
- Quantitative data files containing survey, network, elicitation, and other numerical data

---

It is easy to see that the kinds of files maintained for a project depend on the research questions asked and the purposes of the research; they also depend on the particular preferences and management style of the researcher.

Create a Management System for Interviews, Surveys, and Questionnaires

The steps in creating such a management system include labeling all audio- and videotapes and numbering each

Survey Number (or Tape Number)	Date Transcribed	Name of Transcriber	Date Coded	Name of Coder	Date Entered Into Database
0001	1-15-98	LeCompte	1-25-98	Holloway	1-30-98
0002	1-16-98	LeCompte	1-27-98	Maybin	1-30-98

Figure 3.1. An instrument log.

interview, survey, map, or questionnaire. Researchers also should create a log or notebook for audio- and videotapes, and another log or notebook for interviews, surveys, and questionnaires.

Each instrument or tape should be logged in on a form by its unique identifying number, followed by columns indicating its status, as indicated in Figure 3.1.

Some data may not be coded, and some kinds of surveys and questionnaires may not need to be transcribed. However, it is important to keep track of the dates when notes, instruments, or tapes were handled, and who worked with them, regardless of how the data were manipulated or catalogued. This prevents them from being lost and facilitates monitoring transcribers and coders for accuracy.

Create a Catalog or Index of All Documents and Artifacts

An index makes it possible for research data to be located and retrieved as necessary. Keep the catalog in a place separate from the actual data.

Store All Materials in a Safe Place

Once logs, catalogs, and indexes of data are created, the instruments, tapes, documents, and artifacts themselves can be stored in files and boxes for safekeeping. These boxes should be labeled clearly.

Make a List of All of the Box Labels

Listing all of the box labels creates a complete table of contents of the boxes.

Store Copies and Originals Separately

Storing copies and originals in separate and safe places ensures against theft, loss, fire, and absent-mindedness. It is difficult to overemphasize the need for careful storage of data. It is equally difficult to overemphasize the importance of making copies. The example below spells out some of the disasters that such care can avoid.

EXAMPLE 3.1 ━●━●━

THE IMPORTANCE OF SAFEGUARDING AND DUPLICATING DATA

Ann Nihlen was looking forward to her sabbatical as a time when she would finally turn her dissertation research into a long-awaited book. She moved all of her boxes of original interviews, fieldnotes, and documents from the university into her office at home. One evening, the electrical outlet across the room from her computer short-circuited and caught fire. Flames shot across the room and ignited the piles of data; ultimately, much of the house was badly damaged. Fortunately, Nihlen had kept copies of interviews in her university office, so those data were still intact. When the smoke cleared, she also found that her fieldnotes had been packed so tightly into their boxes that they had burned only part of the way into the files, and much of her data survived—although not the beginnings and endings of files in each box. Her original tapes, journals, and files of documents, however, were completely lost (Nihlen, personal communication, 1997).

Look for Holes or Missing Chunks of Data

Checking for holes requires that the researcher go back to the original research questions, compare them with the actual data collected, and determine if data actually were collected to address each question. Checking for holes is greatly facilitated if the researcher created a data matrix—as illustrated in Book 1, Chapter 6, Figure 6.2. By checking the data planning matrix against the indexes, tables of contents, logbooks of the data collected, and the research questions, missing data problems can be identified. Missing data are not always a problem, however, and even if they are, some data gaps are unavoidable.

Cross Reference: See Book 1, Chapter 6, for an example of a data matrix

Occasionally, researchers decide not to collect data that, although planned for in their original design, turn out to be of little value, or too expensive or difficult to obtain. For example, researchers interested in the extracurricular activities of young adolescents may have little information about what such young people do while skateboarding or in-line skating because the researchers have not learned how to do these things, or they are too old to learn, and they are unable to find a "junior ethnographer" among skateboarders and in-line skaters to collect data in their place. At other times, the research questions are modified so that although some data collection strategies are abandoned, others are added to address questions that were not anticipated initially.

━●━━●━━ EXAMPLE 3.2

MODIFYING ORIGINAL RESEARCH QUESTIONS AND ADDING NEW ONES

In a study of drug use among adolescents and young adults, ethnographer Cristina Huebner discovered that new varieties of marijuana and mixtures of marijuana and other mind-altering substances were available on the streets of Hartford and were being used by young people. Many of these new varieties and mixtures of drugs were not included in drug checklists used in concurrent studies of adult drug users. This discovery resulted in a new set of research questions regarding emerging drug and drug use trends. It produced a "new drugs" interview and a matrix for recording data on these topics as well as on new social arrangements for accessing, using, and dispensing these drugs.

━●━━●━━

Sometimes, a careful review of data and research questions identifies areas that the ethnographer just overlooked. Janet Siskind, an anthropologist studying a group in the Amazon Basin of South America, devoted the early afternoon hours to typing fieldnotes and taking a nap because the unbearable heat made almost any other activity impossible for her. However, the early afternoons were when women did most of their garden work—a very important female activity that provided the staple vegetables upon which families subsisted. Hunting—the male food-gathering activity—was a sporadic event and could not be counted on as a steady source of food. Back at the university, Siskind found that her data were altogether lacking on specifics of what women did in their gardens, but it was impossible for her to return to the field to fill in the gaps (Siskind, 1973). In cases such as these, the ethnographer must explain changes, omissions, gaps, and additions, using whatever theoretical, logistical, or practical rationale is necessary.

Finally, it is important to check on the adequacy of the tidying up process by reading through and reviewing all of the data. Only then can the "real" analysis begin.

SUMMARY

Ethnographers should follow the steps summarized below scrupulously, even if the process seems to divert time from "getting on with the job." Developing systematic records and a workable retrieval system will ensure that data are not lost and that the analysis, interpretation, and write-up of data will be done expeditiously.

Steps in the Tidying Up Process

- Make copies
- Put the fieldnotes in order
- Create an instrument management system
- Catalog all documents and artifacts
- Label and store all data
- Create a table of contents for stored data
- Put copies of data in a safe, separate storage place
- Check for missing data
- Start reading through and reviewing the data

4 ━◆━◆━◆━

ANALYSIS FROM THE TOP DOWN

APPLYING CODES DEDUCTIVELY

Once tidying up has been completed, the masses of accumulated data must be organized and reduced so that the ideas, themes, units, patterns, and structures within them begin to become apparent. This involves a formalized process of analysis, which, in turn, involves some form of **coding** or categorizing data. At the most general level, coding simply means organizing data in terms of a framework that ethnographers can use to support the results and conclusions they reach at the end of their study. At a more specific level, coding can mean actually reading through interviews, fieldnotes, and transcripts and assigning to sentences or paragraphs of text numerical or alphabetic codes representing concepts, categories, or themes.

Methodologists have suggested a number of strategies useful in thinking about, organizing, and coding material in a study. Many ethnographers describe their analysis in somewhat mystical terms, suggesting that themes and patterns emerge from the data as they read their fieldnotes over and over again, somewhat as hikers emerge from the mist on a foggy beach. Unfortunately, *how* these themes and patterns emerge, and what *causes* them to emerge, is left

Definition:
Coding involves organizing data into categories related to the framework and questions guiding the research so that they can be used to support analysis and interpretation

45

unclear. Furthermore, the process of emergence usually is limited to discussions of fieldnotes, leaving out a wide range of other kinds of data, including systematic surveys and questionnaires. Analysis of the entire project requires consideration of *all* of the data collected, as well as triangulation[1] of a variety of kinds of evidence, to achieve credible findings. That is, the themes, patterns, and ideas of interest in a study do not just emerge magically from fieldnotes!

We think that the process of emergence begins with a loose kind of counting process in which the reader of fieldnotes (and the person tallying responses on a survey) observes that certain phrases, events, activities, behaviors, ideas, or other phenomena occur repeatedly in the data. However, as we have pointed out earlier, ethnographers do not just notice these phenomena by chance; in fact, ethnographers are sensitized to specific items and ideas because of the conceptual frameworks within which they work. We would oversimplify the matter if we argued that these conceptual frameworks can be applied either deductively—by choosing a set of concepts first and then sorting out the data in terms of which of the concepts they fit best—or inductively—by examining the data first to see into what kinds of chunks they seem to fall naturally and then choosing a set of concepts that helps to explain why the data fell that way.

 Key point *Such a formulation is an oversimplification because, in fact, ethnographers actually use both induction and deduction throughout their analysis.* However, it is helpful first to explain these procedures separately and then to see how they can be combined. To that end, we begin by looking at more deductive ways of analyzing data, and then we turn to an examination of the more intuitive ways that results begin to emerge from a mass of less structured data.

Deductive analysis can be as simple as dividing data into piles according to their congruity with the principal concepts informing a program that the ethnographer is studying—as in Vadeboncoeur's research, described in Example 4.1—or as complex as applying a list of hundreds of codes to piles of fieldnotes—as was the case in Schensul, Schensul, and Oodit's study of sexual risk in Mauritius (see Example 4.5) or LeCompte's Learning to Work study, an excerpt from whose fieldnotes can be found in Example 2.7 in this book.

➤•➤•➤ **EXAMPLE 4.1**

CODING AT A GENERAL LEVEL: USING A CONCEPTUAL MODEL TO ORGANIZE DATA ABOUT A TEACHER TRAINING PROGRAM

Vadeboncoeur studied the attempts by a U.S. university to restructure its teacher training program. During her fieldwork, Vadeboncoeur came to understand that one of the principal themes of the three-semester program had to do with helping teachers-in-training to become critical thinkers who understood themselves, their own biases and background, and the impact of the social and political environment on their potential students and the schools in which they would teach. She visualized the program as emphasizing three interconnected circles that she called "understanding the self," "understanding other people," and "understanding the environment" (see Figure 4.1). Her database included fieldnotes taken during observations of students in their classes and while they were student teaching, transcripts of interviews conducted with the students and their instructors, a survey she administered to students when they began the program, and the journals that students kept throughout the program. To begin the organization of her data, she used her computer to mark the codes "S" (self), "OP" (other people), and "E" (environment) wherever she found references to self-reflection, comments on the impact of other people, and the influence of the environment in all of the interview transcripts, journals, and fieldnotes of observations. This rough coding gave her a way to examine her data more closely and to separate material that was relevant to the overall themes of her dissertation from other material that—at least at first glance—she did not consider relevant (Vadeboncoeur, 1998).

➤•➤•➤

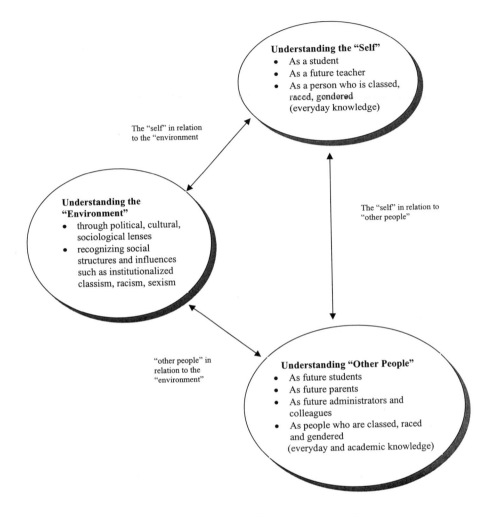

Figure 4.1. A model of emancipatory knowledge (Vadeboncoeur, 1997).

CODING AT A MORE SPECIFIC LEVEL: THE LEARNING TO WORK STUDY

LeCompte (1974, 1978) began her research on the contribution of elementary schooling to children's understanding of the world of work with a pilot study conducted in a community quite distant from her field site. She spent days observing two fourth-grade classrooms and writing down everything the teacher said and did. She then referred to previous studies, as well as to the work of John Dewey, which suggested that the social organization and management structure of classrooms helped to teach children attitudes appropriate for their future lives as citizens and workers. LeCompte read her scripts of teacher behavior over and over, identifying the specific behavior patterns and deportment that the teachers most often tried to instill in their students. These fell into a number of categories that LeCompte termed "Responsibility/Accountability," "Timeliness," "Achievement," "Order," and "Staying on Task." These categories seemed congruent with what the theorists whom her advisors urged her to read had been saying about the impact of schooling, so she tried to arrange as many of the teachers' utterances into these categories. However, arguing that schools were places where children were taught to conform to authority, be on time, remain preoccupied with grades, remain seated, keep working, and be quiet conflicted with ideas that many educational reformers had about the relationship that schools should have with the formation of a democratic society and attitudes about freedom, individualism, and creativity. There also seemed to be no emphasis in these two classrooms on the intrinsic value of learning. So LeCompte added categories such as "Opportunities for Students to Choose Their Own Assignments" and "Valuing Learning for Its Own Sake" that she thought *should* be visible in teacher behavior, even if they were not found in her pilot study. She created a coding system using the initials of the categories and the number of the specific behavior within the list in each category. These behaviors were identified in response to the challenge raised by her advisory committee to create a system so clear that they would be convinced that she would recognize an instance of a category if she saw it. Therefore, codes had to be operationally defined and clear. See Figure 4.2 for a more detailed presentation of the coding categories.

➤●➤●➤

CATEGORY OR DOMAIN: TIME

CODE	OPERATIONAL EXAMPLES
T1A	Visual schedules displayed; notes or reminders for kids' appointments written on the board; reminders of special classes or assignment deadlines written on the board; putting up clock faces as reminders of when to do things
T1B	Cutting off an activity before it's done because of the schedule; talking about "things being messed up" because of the schedule; complaining about things which disrupt the smooth flow of schedule
TIC	Preparatory rituals signaling a new activity; rituals whose purpose is getting ready to do something else
T2A	Statements signaling the end of one activity and beginning of another ("Now put your books away and take out your spellers"); statements telling students when something will be done or what will happen next ("It's time for recess, and after that, we'll do a story")
T2B	Statements which tell students to hurry up or rush and which aren't related to specific tasks
T2C	Nonjudgmental statements about being late ("We're late getting started today, so let's get out our math books")
T2D	Telling a child that an activity is inappropriate for this specific time ("Put the clay away, this is study time" or "You can't talk now, this is quiet time")
T2E	Statements reminding students of emphasized deadlines, when things are due or expected to be finished; queries about a task's status ("Are you done? If you are, you can go outside")
T3A	Punishments or reprimands for being late, handing work in late, or coming in late
T3B	Witholding time for fun as a punishment; taking away recess if a child misbehaves or doesn't do a task; not letting them leave at the end of the day until they are quiet, even if the bell has rung
T3C	Speaking of time as a commodity ("Spend 5 minutes on this," "I'll give you 10 minutes to relax," "Time goes quickly if you use it wisely")

CATEGORY OR DOMAIN: WORK/STAYING ON TASK

W1B	Dispatching orders, short commands telling individual students or small groups what to do. No explanations accompany these orders ("John, finish page 3")
W2A	Get-moving, get-to-work comments designed to get a child working immediately or working harder or faster. They are aimed at accomplishment of a specific activity or task ("Mary, have you nothing to do? Your math is waiting. Come on, you have four problems to do.")
W2B	Moral lectures distinguishing between work and play and on the necessity of work in school. Not used as a reprimand, although it may follow one.
W2C	Descriptive comments that indicate the teacher has observed a student working; meant to encourage others to do so, too ("Boys and girls, George is doing his spelling")
W3A	Detention for not working; losing recess for not working
W3B	Isolation for not working
W3C	Reprimand to individual or group for not working, or for playing

Figure 4.2. Excerpt from coding categories for the Learning to Work study.

LeCompte then put the coding system away and began her four-classroom study. Only when she had finished collecting data did she resurrect the coding system, applying it deductively to her new data set. After coding the entire data set once, she found that she could not classify all of the behaviors of her four teachers using the coding system she had developed during the pilot study. She had to revise the coding system, adding more categories and subcategories and many individual behaviors. She then reapplied the revised system to the data set, generating the results she published for her study. Example 2.7 shows what her coded fieldnotes looked like.

━●━●━ **EXAMPLE 4.3**

CODING DURING FIELDWORK

Angela Smith, a doctoral student at the University of Colorado, noticed that her fellow students seemed to make wide use of humor to defuse the stress of graduate school. For a course project, she explored the kinds and frequency of humor use among her colleagues. She began by asking her fellow students to write down all the kinds of humor that graduate students used, from writing satirical pieces and performing skits that lampooned faculty and staff to teasing, practical jokes, and using irony and puns in their classes. She assembled a list of all of the various uses of humor generated by these brainstorming sessions and created a grid on which she could check off each time that she observed a "humor event." She herself concentrated on coding humor events in the hallways, coffee lounge, and dean's office; during meetings of the Graduate Student Association; and in her own classes throughout the semester. Because she could not be present in each class, she also gave her grid to a representative group of other students, who recorded data for her in their own classes.

━●━●━

These examples demonstrate that coding can be quite holistic, as in Vadeboncoeur's study, where she really only "clumped" the data into three piles, or quite specific, as in

LeCompte's study, in which data were coded in very small segments, usually no longer than a sentence or two. Coding can be used after data are collected, as was the case in LeCompte's and Vadeboncoeur's studies, or during the observation phase, as Smith did, as an actual data collection strategy. All of the above researchers used coding systems that they developed themselves. However, there are many other ways to arrive at coding systems. Frequently, researchers borrow a coding system developed by others at another field site and use it in their own study. Or, they use a system that they developed themselves and apply it to a different population or use it in a different site.

EXAMPLE 4.4   ━●━●━●━

USING THE HUMAN RELATIONS AREA (HRAF) FILES

The HRAF files were developed by anthropologist George Murdock to compile and code ethnographies written by anthropologists and other social scientists anywhere in the world (Murdock, 1971). The coding system he developed enables ethnographers to use a collection of ethnographies that is stored at the Peabody Museum at Yale University. The purpose of the files is to make these ethnographies available for cross-site comparison or for the conduct of meta-analyses or quantitative analyses of qualitative ethnographic data.

A generic coding system was developed consisting of major domains and subdomains representing every possible dimension of cultural, social, economic, and political life (see Figure 4.3). Ethnographies are coded using this system, and the coded chunks stored. The generic coding system is not theoretically based. It has been used by ethnographers working in a variety of different topic areas. The entire coding system is available to ethnographers, but depending upon their topic, studies will use some codes more than others, and many codes will never be used. Ethnographer Bryan Page of the University of Miami Medical School, for example, uses the HRAF files' coding system to code in-depth interviews and observations with injection drug users in central Miami.

━●━●━●━

20. COMMUNICATION
    201. Gestures and Signs
    202. Transmission of Messages
    203. Dissemination of News and Information
    204. Press
    205. Postal System
    206. Telephone and Telegraph
    207. Radio and Television
    208. Public Opinion

34 STRUCTURES
    341. Architecture
    342. Dwellings
    343. Outbuildings
    344. Public Structures
    345. Recreational Structures
    346. Religious and Educational Structures
    347. Business Structures
    348. Industrial Structures
    349. Miscellaneous Structures

46. LABOR
    461. Labor and Leisure
    462. Division of Labor by Sex
    463. Occupational Specialization
    464. Labor Supply and Employment
    465. Wages and Salaries
    466. Labor Relations
    467. Labor Organizations
    468. Collective Bargaining

58. MARRIAGE
    581. Basis of Marriage
    582. Regulation of Marriage
    583. Mode of Marriage
    584. Arranging a Marriage
    585. Nuptials
    586. Termination of Marriage
    587. Secondary Marriages
    588. Irregular Unions
    589. Celibacy

Figure 4.3. Examples of generic codes from HRAF files coding system (from Murdock, 1971).[a]
a. There are, in total, 88 major coding categories in Murdock's scheme.

EXAMPLE 4.5 ━●━●━●━

CODING SEMISTRUCTURED INTERVIEWS WITH YOUNG,
UNMARRIED WOMEN FACTORY WORKERS FROM MAURITIUS

Researchers Schensul, Schensul, and Oodit (1995) guided a team of researchers and health educators to conduct exploratory and semistructured interviews with young women factory workers in Mauritius. Jean Schensul developed a coding system based on a formative theoretical model guiding the study (see Figures 4.4a and 4.4b). The model included three independent domains—family, peers, and work—and two dependent domains—sexual risk behavior, and sexual knowledge, beliefs, and attitudes. Each domain initially was subdivided into between 5 and 10 factors. A semistructured interview schedule was constructed in which one or more open-ended questions was asked for each factor. The initial coding scheme had two levels: domain and factor. When the interviews were reviewed for coding, items or concepts at the subfactor level were developed and added to the coding scheme. The formative ethnographic theory and the fully evolved coding taxonomy for the domain "family" are shown in Figures 4.4a and 4.4b.

━●━●━●━

Cross References: See Book 2, Chapter 7, on structured and semistructured interviewing and observation

The coding system in Figure 4.4b is the final coding system used to code and manage all text data in the "family" domain in the Mauritius Young Women, Work and AIDS study. The coding system includes items at the domain, factor, and subfactor level. The bolded items emerged from key informant interviews and were added to the formative theoretical model portrayed in Figure 4.4a. This revised and enhanced model then guided the development and administration of a semistructured interview schedule. Unbolded factors, subfactors, and variables were added to the conceptual model as a result of semistructured interviews and guided the development of a structured survey instrument described in Book 2, Chapter 8 on survey research.

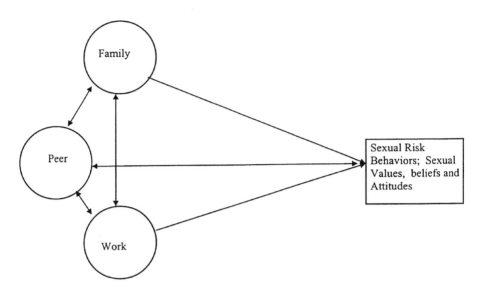

Figure 4.4a. Formative ethnographic theory: Young Women, Work, and AIDS Risk in Mauritius.

WHAT IS A CODE?

Codes are names or symbols used to stand for a group of similar items, ideas, or phenomena that the researcher has noticed in his or her data set. In order to determine the relative frequency of occurrence of items or other phenomena, researchers have to code the data. *For quantitative research, the codes are numerical. When coded, the data can be tabulated or counted for each coding category,* and then the variance that occurs among the various categories can be determined. Usually, codes are given short names that represent, in a somewhat abstracted fashion, the nature of the more concrete items to which they are applied. For example, in the Learning to Work study, LeCompte used the code "Time" whenever the teacher referred to deadlines, schedules, time limits, being on time, or the specific time of

Key point

FAMILY (INDEPENDENT DOMAIN)

FACTOR	SUBFACTOR	VARIABLE (examples)	
FSTRUCTURE	**Family Structure**		
	MAROLE Mother's role	FMCHCARE	Mother's caring for children 16 and under
	FAROLE Father's role	FWKHIST	Father's work history
	FSIZE Family size		
	FSIBS Number of children		
	FBIRTHOR Birth order of young woman		
FMHEALTH	Health of family members		
	FHLTHMO Mother's health status		
	FHLTHFA Father's health status		
	FOTHER Health of other family members		
FWORK	**Family members' work**	FSIBSWK	Siblings work
FVIEWWK	**Family views of work**		
FMAT	Family's attitudes toward peers and social life	FAMATPR	Family's attitudes toward respondent's peers
FMSOC	Family socialization practices with respondent	FAMTALK	Family members discuss issues with respondent
FMACTIV	Family activities with young woman		
FMPROB	Family problems		
FWHYWORK	Reasons for going to work	FSELFINC	Work for personal income
		FFAMINC	Work for household income

Figure 4.4b. Coding tree example: Young Women, Work and AIDS Study, Mauritius.

day. Similarly, Vadeboncoeur coded under the category "Self" all stories that students told about their personal experience, any instances where students judged the behavior of other people by their own personal value systems, or whenever they held up their own background as the standard by which other experiences should be evaluated.

WHAT DO CODES LOOK LIKE?

Codes have the following characteristics:

- They are **operational**. Codes are applied to items in the data that respond to the statement "An 'X' [name of code] looks like this!"

- They have names, often a single term (such as sex, coded as male or female) or a phrase such as "showing respect for elders" (demonstrated by the presence of behaviors such as standing in the presence of elders, speaking politely to elders, offering assistance to elders, and doing what elders tell one to do) or "dropping out of school" (measured by factors such as the fact that a student has exceeded the permitted number of unexcused absences, is not currently attending school, and has no plans to return to school).

- Their names are close to the concept they describe, and they are *not* numbers. Code names can be a point on a scale, a discrete concrete item, a person, a kind of event, an idea, a theme, or any number of other things.

- Individual code names are distinctly different from one another.

- Codes must be kept at a low **level of inference**, at least in the initial stages of coding. This helps keep the coded items discrete from one another and avoids the unreliability involved when coders have to make too many value judgments about how to classify items. Such judgments can vary because of the differences in coders' backgrounds and biases, so coders who must do high inference coding must be well trained initially, or their work will be inconsistent and unreliable. Low inference descriptors used to describe a house could include (Code A) peeling paint, (Code B) holes in the roof, (Code C) broken

Definition:
Operational codes mark items or units in the data that are measureable and have observable boundaries

Cross Reference:
See Book 2, Chapter 2, for continua reflecting levels of inference and abstraction

Definition:
Level of inference refers to the degree of interpretation or evaluation done by the coder; low inference coding stays very close to actual concrete description

windows, and (Code D) torn window screens. Codes used later in the analytic process can be at a higher level of inference or abstraction; using the example of the house above, codes could include (Code A) really old, or (Code B) deteriorated, or (Code C) both old and deteriorated based on the coder's intepretation of the descriptions recorded in data. *As we noted earlier, high-inference coding requires greater attention to training of coders to ensure that judgments are consistent across all coders.*

- Codes are related to naturally occurring chunks or items or units of analysis, if possible. These can be paragraphs; units of time (hours, minutes, days, weeks); specific utterances; observable behaviors; and so on. For example, LeCompte called her chunks of data "verbal episodes" and defined them as all of those words, sentences, or even paragraphs between the beginning and end of a distinct topic. Most of the time, the verbal episodes were limited to several sentences or phrases, but some, such as minilectures on some serious misbehavior on the part of the students or complicated sets of instructions for a coming activity, were quite lengthy.

- Codes used for surveys and questionnaires should include analytically separate codes for (a) answers that were not obtained or are missing or undecipherable; (b) situations in which the questions did not apply or were not relevant to the informant (such as asking "Have you ever been pregnant?" of a male respondent or a very young child); and (c) situations in which the respondent says that he or she does not know the answer to the question.

- Codes should reduce data to a manageable form, not expand it. Therefore, they should subsume or place into larger groups many smaller items or groups of items, as was the case in Vadeboncoeur's and LeCompte's studies described earlier.

- Codes are often organized hierarchically and can be thought of as branching tree diagrams, with sub-subcodes collapsing into subcodes, which are then subsumed into larger codes. Figures 4.4a, 4.4b, and 4.5 illustrate this type of organization.

WHERE DO CODES COME FROM?

We already have indicated that researchers often borrow coding systems from other researchers or from studies they

 Key point

 Definition: High-inference coding involves interpretation and requires that the coder make judgments as to which code is more appropriate; high-inference codes are the building blocks of analysis, interpretation, and theory generation, and they are sometimes called theoretical memos (Glaser & Strauss, 1967)

 Cross References: See Books 1 and 2 for a discussion of how to identify and define units of analysis

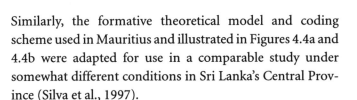

have already done themselves. They also frequently adapt an existing set of coding categories that they or someone else has developed.

EXAMPLE 4.6

ADAPTATION OF A PREVIOUSLY USED CODING SYSTEM

LeCompte adapted the coding categories for "Responsibility," "Accountability," "Time," "Task Orientation," "Opportunities for the Students to Direct Their Own Instruction," and "Taking Initiative" from the Learning to Work study for use in her study of the Arts Focus Program (see Figure 6.1). Even though the former study was done with elementary school children in regular classes and Arts Focus was a middle school arts program, the teachers still placed great emphasis on these specific norms, and the categories fit the Arts Focus data very well.

Similarly, the formative theoretical model and coding scheme used in Mauritius and illustrated in Figures 4.4a and 4.4b were adapted for use in a comparable study under somewhat different conditions in Sri Lanka's Central Province (Silva et al., 1997).

Coding categories can come from quite mundane sources. One of the most common sets of categories are the demographic categories used by the U.S. Bureau of the Census and other mass survey organizations to delineate the general characteristics of a population. These include categories such as age, sex, race or ethnicity, educational level, occupation, income, place of residence, religious preference, and political party preference. Often, these categories actually constitute the variables that structure the hypotheses that the researcher wants to test or the research questions of interest in the study. For example, "Does instruction in the arts have a greater impact on the identity formation of *boys* or *girls*?" or "Why is it that arts education programs enroll so few *males, minority* students, and *poor* students—even when the programs are located in public schools and require no special fees?" or "In which kinds of *communities* are *minority* school dropouts most likely to live: the inner city, city borders, the suburbs, or in rural areas?" In the above questions, the coding categories are sex, ethnicity, social class—probably measured in terms of the educational level, income level, and occupation of the students' parents—and place of residence. At least some of this kind of information customarily is included with every survey, test instrument, interview, or questionnaire so as to maintain information on possible variation within a population.

Rough deductive coding categories also can be derived from the conceptual and theoretical frames or research questions around which the researcher built the study, as was the case in Vadeboncoeur's study.

EXAMPLE 4.7   ━●━●━●━

BUILDING A CODING SYSTEM DEDUCTIVELY FROM A CONCEPTUAL FRAMEWORK

Vadeboncoeur (1997) had hypothesized—and administrators of the teacher training program she studied hoped—that over the three-semester sequence of professional seminar courses that she studied for her dissertation, teacher-training students would develop more and more sophisticated explanations for why public school students succeeded or failed in their studies. Vadeboncoeur conceptualized developmental growth as a movement from a preoccupation with "self" to more cognizance of the influence of "other people," and finally to a recognition of the impact that "the environment," or structural forces—such as social class, patterns of discrimination, economic disparities, and academic ability grouping in schools—could have on students' chances for success. To that end, Vadeboncoeur sorted her coded data into three other piles according to the semester in which the specific pieces of data were collected. By plotting the relative incidence of codes in each category by semester, she was able to get a rough idea of how and whether the students' descriptions changed over time and, as well, to learn to what any observed changes could be attributed. She displayed her data in a table arranged as in Figure 4.5.

━●━●━●━

	Student Name	Semester One	Semester Two	Semester Three
"Self"	Dale Sue Cary Ella	# of examples from data for each student	# of examples from data for each student	# of examples from data for each student
"Other People"	Dale Sue Cary Ella	# of examples from data for each student	# of examples from data for each student	# of examples from data for each student
"The Environment"	Dale Sue Cary Ella	# of examples from data for each student	# of examples from data for each student	# of examples from data for each student

Figure 4.5. Student development over time.

PRECODING DATA

Some of the easiest data to crunch are those that have been collected in a form that can be counted or enumerated. Sometimes, researchers like to begin their analysis with this material because the analysis is quite straightforward and the yields—in terms of results—are rather immediate. This can help make the ethnographer feel as though progress is being made even though the fieldnotes have not yet been analyzed. Easy or **precoded data** can include enumerated (or numerical) data, such as test scores, purchase records, attendance figures, and so on; or so-called nominal data, which involve specific, named categories of things, such as sex (male, female); province or state of residence; political party affiliation (Christian Democrat, Socialist, Green, Labor); and to which churches or religious organizations respondents belong. Interviews and all standardized surveys and questionnaires contain responses that consist primarily of material that has been precoded in this way; that is, the material consists of answers to closed-ended questions. Many have built-in coding systems that, once applied, yield categories of things that can be readily counted, such

Definition: Precoded data are data that have been categorized so that a given number or letter represents a single kind of information about a given person, group, setting, or other researcher-defined unit of analysis

as sex; age; preference for particular kinds of food or entertainment; places of residence; and estimated frequencies of
specific types of behavior, such as drug use or number of
household moves.

KINDS OF CODES OR CATEGORIES

Descriptive codes are those most commonly used in precoded instruments. They include such things as whether or
not a person is enrolled in school; an injection drug user;
the parent of a student enrolled in a particular educational
program; a lover of classical music; a known sufferer from
hypertension or diabetes; or whether or not they have ever
had cancer, a hysterectomy, or a tooth extraction. The answer to all of these questions usually is unambiguously yes
or no; "yes" can be coded as a "one" and "no" as a "two,"
and all of the yesses and nos can be counted to give the
researcher some idea of the profile of participants. Such
dichotomous variables, or kinds of information that have
only two options, can include demographic information
such as sex (male or female) and whether or not a person
owns a personal computer (yes or no). LeCompte and
Holloway used such a question as part of an instrument
assessing parents' opinions about the Arts Focus program
(see Figure 4.6). Other kinds of variables, such as the number of homes, cars, or telephones a person owns, or the
number of times people attend concerts, purchase prescrip-
tion drugs, or take trips away from their home community,
can be recorded in actual numbers.

 **Cross
Reference:**
See Chapter 8,
this book, for
a discussion
of different types
of variables

Other types of descriptive data can be grouped so that
the possible answers can be coded by numbers. Such information includes such things as political party (Republican,
Democratic, Socialist, Socialist Worker, Green, Liberal) or
religious affiliation (Protestantism, Catholicism, Judaism,

9. Do you think Arts Focus has helped your child:

Learn to be more disciplined	Yes _____ or No _____
Engage in sustained efforts	Yes _____ or No _____
Develop a capacity for healthy self-critique	Yes _____ or No _____
Perform or display his/her work in public	Yes _____ or No _____
Take risks	Yes _____ or No _____
Collaborate with others on projects	Yes _____ or No _____
Think of alternative ways of doing or thinking about things	Yes _____ or No _____
Solve problems	Yes _____ or No _____
Develop the ability to express him/herself	Yes _____ or No _____
Develop self-confidence	Yes _____ or No _____
Take responsibility for his/her work and duties	Yes _____ or No _____

Figure 4.6. Dichotomous questions from the Arts Focus Parent Questionnaire.

Buddhism, Islam, Hinduism, Shintoism, etc.); occupation (professional, managerial, educational, clerical, service, technical, manual, agricultural, child care, homecare, unemployed); educational level (see the following list); and place of residence (inner city, periurban, suburban, semirural, and rural).

As we have noted in Books 1 and 2, creating *valid* precoded instruments—that is, instruments whose language and concepts make sense to the person who is being interviewed or surveyed—requires a lot of preliminary fieldwork. This is because the options or codes that researchers use in their instruments have to include all of the options or information that reasonable informants would think of in trying to answer the questions. For example, researchers interested in the educational levels of participants could have them record the exact number of years they attended school or permit them to choose among the following options:

_____ Never attended school

_____ Attended some primary school (Grades kindergarten through 6)

_____ Completed primary school (completed Grade 6)

_____ Attended some secondary school (Grades 7-12)

_____ Completed secondary school (completed Grade 12)

_____ Attended some college or postsecondary institution

_____ Graduated from a college or postsecondary institution

_____ Attended some postbaccalaureate or graduate institution

_____ Graduated from a postbaccalaureate or graduate institution

Definition:
A scale is a way to record both the direction and the intensity of a person's feeling about or opinions on a specific thing

Cross Reference:
See Book 5, Chapter 8, on different types of variables; and Book 2, for ways of creating prestructured questions

Still another kind of descriptive data involves people's opinions and attitudes about any number of things. Such information cannot be measured unambiguously, but people usually can estimate how strongly they feel about events or phenomena if they are given a range from which to choose. These estimates can be recorded on **scales**, expressed in degrees of feeling, and recorded as a rank ordering of numbers that constitutes the precoded answers that the researcher uses to analyze the data. For example, researchers could ask people about their current health status (1 = *excellent*, 2 = *very good*, 3 = *average*, 4 = *poor*, 5 = *very poor*); their enthusiasm about an educational program for their children (1 = *very enthusiastic*, 2 = *moderately enthusiastic*, 3 = *neutral*, 4 = *unenthusiastic*, 5 = *very unenthusiastic*); or their willingness to attend a disease prevention seminar (1 = *very interested*, 2 = *moderately interested*, 3 = *not interested*). LeCompte and Holloway used the scale shown in Figure 4.7 in their Arts Focus Study.

LIMITATIONS ON CODING

Codes do not tell us everything; for example, knowing how many years a person went to school would not tell a researcher if specific individuals repeated grades or attended part-time, or the kinds of institutions in which they en-

8. Please rate the effectiveness of each characteristic of the Arts Focus Program. Circle an appropriate number:

	Not Effective			Extremely Effective	
Scheduling	1	2	3	4	5
Range of activities in the classroom	1	2	3	4	5
Types of instruction	1	2	3	4	5
Skill of teacher	1	2	3	4	5
Personality of teacher	1	2	3	4	5
Quality of guest artists	1	2	3	4	5
Quality of fieldtrips	1	2	3	4	5
Quality and quantity of supplies, resources, and equipment	1	2	3	4	5
Level of administrative support	1	2	3	4	5
Level of overall funding for Arts Focus	1	2	3	4	5
Level of involvement of Arts Focus parents	1	2	3	4	5

Are there other qualities you'd like to evaluate? Please list and rate them.

Figure 4.7. A precoded scaled measurement: "Please rate the effectivness."

rolled. Similarly, researchers could not tell from the codes above whether an individual attended or graduated from a 2-year college, a 4-year university, a postsecondary technical/vocational school, or a secretarial institute. Indeed, the codes above might not make sense to individuals who had received certificates from 1- or 2-year technical or clerical institutes and did not know how to classify them. Further fieldwork might be needed to make sure that the categories included all of the possible responses. Questions about *willingness* to attend a seminar or participate in a program will not tell the researcher if people actually *did* attend. Additional questions—and perhaps some observations at such programs or seminars—might be needed to determine fine points. However, precoding can be refined and certainly permits researchers to make rough descriptions of a population in a relatively short period of time by showing how many people fall into each category of a given code. In short, when done well, such instruments permit us to learn very efficiently a considerable amount of information about a great many people.

SUMMARY

Coding from the top down can begin with theories and hypotheses, as was the case in Vadeboncoeur's study, in which the theories that guided her research also were the basis of her initial coding or "clumping" categories: Self, Other, and the Environment. By contrast, coding can be associate with little theory at all, as is the case for the precoded demographic data that researchers always collect as a way to identify categories of respondents. However, these same theoryless categories can come in quite handy when researchers need to explore the strength of a theory with regard to a particular group or set of individuals. In all of these cases, however, the codes are applied on top of the data, whether the application is done during the data collection phases of research or after the data are all collected. In the next chapter, we discuss inductive coding, in which codes first must be identified; only then can they be applied to various forms of data.

NOTE

1. Triangulation, which we define in Books 1 and 2, is the use of data from two or more different sources (or several different kinds of data) to corroborate what an informant has said or what an ethnographer has concluded.

5 ◆━◆━◆━◆

ANALYSIS FROM THE BOTTOM UP: THE ITEM LEVEL OF ANALYSIS

In the discussion so far, we have assumed that the researcher began his or her study with a set of preexisting codes or at least developed a set of codes before the actual "crunching" process began. Most ethnography, however, even if it begins with a formative research model, does not start with preexisting codes. The vast majority of the data collected are not numerical or already coded because, with the exception of ethnographic surveys, ethnographers collect words, not numbers. Those words make up descriptions of observations, fieldnotes, quotations, transcripts, books and articles, elicitation data, documents, and excerpts from interviews. As the noted analysts Matthew Miles and A. M. Huberman (1984, p. 54) have said, words are fatter than numbers; they have multiple and sometimes ambiguous meanings, and they have little meaning without context, whether that context is as simple as the words immediately preceding and following a word or phrase of interest, or as complex as the complete event in which it was uttered. The problem faced by ethnographers is that they must somehow clump words together; organize and classify or code them in a systematic way; and, in some instances, translate them into numbers for quantitative analysis.

We already have noted that ethnographers sometimes speak of how their results emerge from qualitative data as if the emergence were a kind of mystical process. Although seemingly mysterious, the emergence of patterns actually occurs because the researcher is engaged in a systematic inductive thought process that clumps together individual items at the specific level into more abstract statements about the general characteristics of those items as a group. This inductive process facilitates the transformation of words into coded items that then can be ranked, ordered, or counted in what Miles and Huberman call "arithmetic." Following arithmetic, ethnographers begin to assemble the items into patterns and structures.

We believe that this process takes place in three stages, which can be called the "item," "pattern," and "constitutive" or "structural" levels of analysis. These can be thought of as different levels of abstraction in which

Cross Reference: See Book 2, Chapter 2, and Book 5, Chapter 8, for tables and discussion summarizing these levels

- "Items" consist of discrete and concrete units of analysis or things—the specific units that one codes
- "Patterns" consist of collections of items or categories of items that seem to fit together or are related to one another
- "Constituents" or "structures" consist of larger groups of patterns or relationships among patterns in the data that begin to build an overall cultural portrayal or theory explaining a cultural phenomenon

THE ITEM LEVEL OF ANALYSIS

Before researchers can produce scientifically supportable interpretations of their data, they have to isolate specific items or elements that are related to the research questions. Items are "units"; they are similar to the codes we have defined earlier in this chapter. Item-level analysis involves identifying in data sources those things that must be coded before they can be counted or measured, in a process similar to Vadeboncoeur's examination of change in student perceptions over time, depicted in Figure 4.5. The identification of items helps researchers make sense of what otherwise would be an undifferentiated morass of information. After researchers have laboriously looked over, read repeatedly, tidied up (Romagnano, 1991), and organized their data, the inductive process begins to produce items in the form of those events, behaviors, statements, or activities that stand out because they occur often; are crucial to other items; are rare and influential; or are totally absent, despite the researcher's expectations.

LeCompte and Preissle (1993, p. 239) call the processes that researchers use to identify items (or patterns and structures, for that matter) **theorizing.** In Book 2, Schensul, Schensul, and LeCompte refer to a similar process as *building formative theory.* We believe that theorizing—or building formative theory—resembles the kind of thinking that people do in everyday life—except that theorizing is done in a more systematic manner. It starts with the laborious and time-consuming tasks of pulling apart fieldnote narratives, interviews, and documents; identifying relevant information from them; matching that information with relevant information from other sources of data, such as maps, surveys, and questionnaires; and then trying to figure out why they fit together as they do. The cognitive processes involved are

Definition: Theorizing is the "cognitive process of discovering abstract categories and the relationships among them; it is used to develop or confirm explanations for how and why things happen as they do" (LeCompte & Preissle, 1993, p. 239)

- Perceiving
- Comparing
- Contrasting
- Aggregating
- Ordering
- Establishing linkages and relationships
- Speculating

As we described earlier, researchers take a series of steps in creating, recreating, and refining conceptual models. They

- Notice the phenomona around them
- Differentiate these phenomena from each other by comparing and contrasting them with past experiences, sets of values, or predetermined conceptual frameworks or theories
- Select those that they feel are most important for further examination
- Organize them into conceptual taxonomies or hierarchies of abstraction—domains, factors, subfactors, variables
- Identify which variables, factors, and, eventually, domains are associated with one another
- Develop explanations for these associations

Item-level analysis is used at any and all points in the analytical process. The process is used to expand and further develop formative theoretical models by identifying new domains, factors, variables, and items. Item-level analysis can even be reintroduced after the study is over if researchers are revisiting the ethnographic database with new questions and domains of interest. For this reason, we pay special attention to item-level analysis in this chapter.

A number of theorists, including Spradley (1979), Glaser and Strauss (1967), Lofland (1971), Lofland and Lofland (1984) and Mishler (1986) have tried to systematize procedures for facilitating item-level analysis.

USING DOMAIN ANALYSIS TO IDENTIFY ITEMS

Definition: Domain analysis is a strategy for identifying and differentiating classes of items in a culture

One of the most useful strategies for playing with ideas was developed by James Spradley, a noted methodologist, who called the strategy he used for identifying items "domain analysis." This kind of analysis is initiated using what are called descriptive questions, which induce people to describe the components of the world in which they live—

for example, "family," "games," "activities," or "work." Weller and Romney (1988) refer to this and other elicitation tools, including listings, taxonomies, sentence completions, and triad sorts, as "systematic data collection." The components identified through systematic data collection often are called "domains," which consist of large units of cultural knowledge. Domains are classes of objects, things, ideas, or events in the real world, or at least in the world as people understand it and perceive it to be. Each domain in a study is given a distinct domain name. *Symbols* in Spradley's system are the smaller units of which domains are composed; they have no real meaning other than that which people give to them. Symbols often have concrete referents or meanings, however. For example, the word symbol "mouse" refers to or denotes a small rodent, but the same word symbol can also mean part of the auxiliary equipment necessary for operating a personal computer, or the discolored tissue around the eye that results when a person runs into a door or is punched in the face. Symbols can have a wide variety of connotative meanings independent of their denotative or referential meaning. For example, a mouse *is* a small rodent (or a small plastic piece of electronic equipment or a black eye), but to many people, it *connotes* filth or something terrifying. A large rodent *is* a rat, but "rat" also refers in English to a person who double-crosses or deceives others. "To rat" also is a verb meaning the procedure used by hairdressers to tangle women's hair into a mass that creates the illusion of much more hair than women actually have. For many young teenagers, "college" connotes more than its denotative meaning of "an institution of higher learning." College, or going to college, can also symbolically represent independence, because going to college can mean leaving one's parents' home and becoming an adult. Ethnographers need to engage in sufficient fieldwork to ensure that they understand all of the various connotative and denotative meanings possessed by the symbols that their

Cross Reference: See Book 3, Borgatti's chapter, for a discussion of more systematic methods for eliciting cultural domains

research participants use, prior to organizing these units into domains. Ethnographers can code their data by domain, by subdomain, or by factor, depending on how abstract the domain is and how detailed the coding system is.

Domains are categories or arrays of distinct things that ethnographers—or informants—treat as related to one another in some way and existing at more or less the same level of abstraction. The ethnographer must elicit the relevant symbols in the world of his or her informants and then, during the analysis phase of the research project, organize them into domains. Determining the relationships and equivalent levels of abstraction is not always easy or straightforward; symbols may have the same referent but different connotative meanings. For example, the word symbols "juvenile," "young person," and "adolescent" can have the same denotative meaning, but for many people, the terms "juvenile" and "adolescent" can have negative connotations. "Juvenile" can be associated with delinquent behavior and "adolescent" with naive or foolhardy actions. Similarly, whereas the cover term "plants" could apply to such things as seaweed, oaks, forests, palm trees, cacti, roses, grain, living organisms, tea, and rice, it is clear that the above list of "plants" consists of many varied things at several levels of abstraction, none of which is very much like any other except at the most general level.

James Spradley called the names given to domains "cover terms." Cover terms simply are the most inclusive or general term that can be applied to the array of things included in a given domain. Any given domain consists of "included terms," or the names for those things subsumed by the domain. For example, cover terms could be "trees," "musicians," and "ways to annoy a professor"; some of the associated included terms could include those displayed in Figure 5.1. We refer to this process, when it occurs in the early stages of the research for purposes of guiding it, as "vertical modeling."

Cross Reference:
See Book 2, Chapters 2 and 3, for a discussion of theorizing, building formative theory, and operationalizing

COVER TERM	"TREES"	"MUSICIANS"	"WAYS TO ANNOY PROFESSORS"
Included terms	Oaks, palms, banyans, elms, bamboos, pines, etc.	Pianist, guitarist, harpist, violinist, singer, etc.	Turn papers in late, chat in class, forget your book, arrive late to class, etc.

Figure 5.1. Cover terms and included terms for domains.

Initially, the category "musician" could include the terms "singer," "professional," "amateur," "orchestra player," or "band member." Although all of these terms could apply to people who are musicians, only the term "singer" is at the same level as the ones in Figure 5.1, because all of the latter terms refer to the specific instrument that the musician plays—and a singer's instrument is his or her voice. One of the most important things the domain analyst does, then, is to establish the boundaries of the domain by using rules that permit the ethnographer to make distinctions between what is and is not included in the domain. These boundaries are identified by looking for the way that the items are connected by semantic relationships. Semantic relationships are stated in the form of sentences, as indicated in Figure 5.2. Of course, there can be other semantic relationships; we list only some of the most common.

Cross Reference: See Borgatti's chapter in Book 3 for a discussion of hierarchical relationships in domains

Domains can include subdomains. For example, musical instruments are a domain that includes violins; violins are a domain that includes modern and baroque violins; modern violins are a domain that includes violins made after 1900 and violins made at any time since the 1600s that have been modernized.

Figure 5.3 illustrates part of a taxonomy that LeCompte developed in the Learning to Work study. LeCompte identified two principal categories of noninstructional verbal behavior in which teachers engaged: Management Behavior and Discretionary Behavior (see Figure 10.11 for a Venn

Form	Relationship
x is a kind of y	Strict inclusion
x is a place in y, x is a part of y	Spatial
x is a result of y; x is a cause of y	Cause-effect
x is a reason for doing y	Rationale
x is a place for doing y	Location for action
x is used for y	Function
x is a way to do y	Means-end
x is a step or stage in y	Sequence
x is a characteristic of y	Attribution
x can be found in y	Location

Figure 5.2. Types of semantic relationships (adapted from Spradley, 1979).

diagram of how these domains were linked to each other). Management Behavior, in turn, was composed of behavior categorized into three subdomains: Time, Work (or Staying on Task), and Responsibility (or Conformity to Authority). These, in turn, were composed of sub-subdomains of individual behaviors, which were coded as illustrated in Example 2.7 and Figure 4.2. In Figure 5.3, a domain is made up of management behavior that LeCompte observed in all four of the classrooms she studied; the subdomains are Work, Time, and Responsibility. The letters and numbers in the sub-subdomains represent specific behaviors; some letters and numbers in the sequence are missing (e.g., "W1A" and "W2C"); these represented behaviors that were hypothesized to exist prior to fieldwork, but that did not occur in the classrooms LeCompte observed. They were omitted in the final analysis of data. Furthermore, some subdomains are represented by a greater number of coded behaviors than others; this is because the structure of some domains is more complex than others.

Taxonomies such as the one in Figure 5.3 visually represent the hierarchical ordering of items as well as the linkages and relationships among various items in a domain. They not only help to classify information, but they can be a

Cross Reference: See Book 2, Chapters 2 and 3, for a more detailed discussion of this process

DOMAIN	MANAGEMENT CORE		
SUBDOMAIN	TIME	WORK	RESPONSIBILITY
SUB-SUBDOMAINS	T1A	W1B	R1A
	T1B	W2A	R1B
	T1C	W2B	R1C
	T1D	W2D	R2A
	T2A	W3A	R2B
	T2B	W3B	R2C
	T2C	W3C	R2D
	T2D	W1B1	R2E
	T3A	W1B2	R2F
	T3B		R2G
	T3C		R3
	T1A1		R4A
	T1A2		R1A1
			R1B1

Figure 5.3. Domains, subdomains, sub-subdomains: A taxonomy.

critical first step in identifying structures in the cultural life of whatever group an ethnographer studies.

USING CONSTANT COMPARISON AND ANALYTIC INDUCTION TO IDENTIFY ITEMS

One of the most well-known strategies for identifying items was initially spelled out by Barney Glaser and Anselm Strauss (1965) in a study of death and dying in a hospital. They called their strategy "constant comparison." Glaser and Strauss wanted to know at what point a person was, in the minds of those who had known him or her, truly deceased, and if these different definitions had any impact on the behavior of the deceased person's health care workers and family.

They began by studying how the way in which doctors, nurses, and other health care personnel talked about patients who were terminally ill changed as those patients moved through stages from being very ill, to death, and finally to removal from the hospital for burial. They noticed, for example, that patients who had died within the past few hours were still described in the present tense, as if they were still living. The researchers kept careful records of the names or identifiers that different kinds of health care workers applied to patients at varying stages of their illness, reasoning that aides and nurses would have different jobs—and therefore different relationships to patients—that might affect how they defined—and therefore described—the dying person. They constantly compared the language used by one set of workers with that of the others, as well as the language used to describe patients in one stage of illness with that used to describe patients in other stages. In the process of comparison, they looked for similarities and differences in behaviors, settings, actors, and other dimensions of cultural life and made inferences about these differences. The thinking process in constant comparison is very similar to that required in quantitative data analysis when researchers explore differences in, for example, educational performance or compliance with medical treatment by gender, ethnicity, age, socioeconomic status, or other factors.

The process of constant comparison permitted Glaser and Strauss to develop a set of consistent identifiers that marked the stages of life from serious illness to death and that also denoted the social worth—as measured by the kind of treatment and the level of respect implied in the names applied to those various stages of life—of individuals in each stage. Glaser and Strauss also recorded the way that these identifiers denoted a form of progressive distancing used by medical personnel to protect them from too much intimacy with patients whom they knew would soon die.

The organization of Glaser and Strauss's analysis is similar to, and not incompatible with, Spradley's domain analysis: The stream of behavior or language is recorded and then separated into discrete concepts using constant comparison. The items are then "chunked" into categories. Subsequent steps link the categories into concepts or theoretical constructs that, in turn, permit selection or development of theories that the researcher can use to explain what was observed in the field. Table 5.1, shown at the end of the chapter, displays a comparison of the stages in the principal forms of analysis reviewed in this book, showing their similarities and differences.

A specialized form of comparison used in all forms of analysis is **analytic induction;** we include it here because it is a specialized form of comparison. Its principal feature is its emphasis on a search for negative or disconfirming cases. Researchers find it easier to look for items that are similar to what they have just identified as being of interest in a study; similarity, after all, tends to confirm a researcher's insights. However, Florian Znaniecki, a Polish sociologist who based his book about the experiences of Polish immigrants in the United States on an analysis of letters that immigrants wrote to family members remaining in Poland (Znaniecki, 1930), cautioned researchers not to ignore the negative case, or the one that is dissimilar to the majority of cases or items found so far in a study. In some ways, negative cases serve to protect researchers from excess enthusiasm about the credibility of their initial findings. They also help researchers to refine the definitions of their items and categories; negative cases alert researchers to variance within a population and to nuances and dimensions of meaning and perception that would be ignored were a systematic search for such differences not done.

Systematic analytic induction also helps the researcher identify omissions, not only of items, ideas, events, behaviors, and so on that investigators thought might or should be present, but also those absences that researchers do not anticipate. For example, in the early stages of the AIDS epidemic, the absence in the United States of cases of women infected with HIV/AIDS led researchers to define

Definition:
Analytic induction refers to the identification of negative or disconfirming cases

Cross Reference:
See Book 2, Chapter 10, for a discussion of spurious conclusions and their threat to validity

the disease as one affecting only homosexual men. As a consequence, when some women did begin to exhibit AIDS symptoms, their illness was misdiagnosed. In other countries, however, HIV/AIDS afflicted both men and women. Had researchers looked beyond the U.S. data, or had they looked closely at the improbability that an infectious disease would afflict only one sex, they might have identified more clearly the nature of the disease.

USING LOFLAND'S STRUCTURE OF ACTIVITIES TO IDENTIFY ITEMS

John Lofland's (1971) and John and Lyn Lofland's (1984) analyses focus more narrowly on the structure of human interaction. They move from a rather microscopic examination of the constituents and details of human interaction to a more macroscopic perspective on how those constituents are aggregated into the behavior and beliefs of larger groups. Rather than beginning with a process of item identification, as is the case with both Spradley and Glaser and Strauss, Lofland and Lofland's strategy begins with a hierarchically organized set of categories:

- Acts and Actors
- Activities
- Settings
- Ways of Participating
- Relationships
- Meanings

This is roughly parallel to the categories suggested by Pelto and Pelto in observing, documenting, and categorizing field situations (Pelto & Pelto, 1978). Although researchers could begin with any of the first four categories (acts, actors, activities, and settings), the Loflands' approach involves first identifying all of the individual actors in a particular setting, as well as the acts in which they are engaged. The researcher might do this for several settings encompassed by the research site. In the Learning to Work study, for example, LeCompte observed students and teachers (actors) in classrooms, on the playground, in the library, and at lunch in the cafeteria (settings). She then worked to identify the acts and activities in which the actors engaged in each of these settings. The Loflands define "acts" as small-scale interactions in which individuals are engaged, and that conduce to one specific goal. Individual acts can be combined into activities. For example, you, the reader of this book, are currently engaged in the act of reading. When you stop reading, you will do so to engage in other acts, such as hearing the telephone ring, rising from your chair, walking across the room to the telephone, picking up the phone receiver, and uttering a greeting. Taken together, the last four acts constitute part of an activity called "talking on the telephone" in which you (an actor) are engaged with a friend, family member, colleague, or some other actor.

Actors participate in settings in different ways; some actors may read best with a television or radio turned on for background noise; others need silence. Some may prefer to slouch in a comfortable chair; others need a chair and writing desk for taking notes. The participative style may also depend on the relationship that the actor has with the particular book and the reasons why it is being read: A book read for schoolwork will be more likely to require the chair and desk. This is because the relationship that the actor has with the book is different from the relationship that the actor has with a friend who recommended it, and the set of meanings attached to that relationship dictate different ways of interacting and participating. Lofland suggests that an outline of the structure of activity be developed first, followed by a systematic search for the meanings that people attach to their activities, relationships, and ways of participating. Strategies such as those outlined in Book 2,

Cross Reference: See Book 2, Chapters 4, 5, and 6, and Book 4 for more discussion on ways of collecting information on activities, actors, and relationships in space and time and in Borgatti's chapter on elicitation techniques found in Book 3, are helpful in eliciting such meanings.

USING MISHLER'S LINGUISTIC ANALYSIS TO IDENTIFY ITEMS IN STORIES

Elliot Mishler (1986), a sociolinguist, focuses on the analysis of texts—in particular, texts created from interviews or stories told by informants. Mishler recognizes that the stories people tell during an interview often do not make sense without some kind of rewriting by the researcher. They may lack any kind of chronological or logical order; they may jump around, addressing various topics in a nearly random manner; and they may stretch over several different interviews conducted at different times. It is the researcher's job to reorganize the information so that it can serve as evidence in support of whatever propositions the researcher is exploring in an investigation. Mishler suggests first restructuring the interview in a narrative form, one that resembles the story form of Western literature. This means orienting the reader to the time and place of the story; identifying the people (or characters) involved in the story; describing what happened (the drama or plot); identifying the resolution of the plot (or how it all turned out); and, finally, giving an evaluation or indication of how the storyteller felt about the events covered in the story itself.

Once these procedures are followed, Mishler argues that the researcher can identify the critical elements in the story, telling which ones predicted change in the events or behavior of individual characters; categorize the content of the story and indicate the function that each category performs; discuss the meanings in the story; and then connect those meanings to more global assumptions or worldviews held by individuals or within the culture under study.

SUMMARY

In this chapter, we have reviewed a series of inductive strategies for generating items and codes from data and then assembling them into patterns. Each of these strategies yields a slightly different perspective on the data and, taken together, produces the sets of patterns that ethnographers then assemble into a more complete portrait of the cultural scene they are investigating. Table 5.1 arrays six different analytic schemes developed by LeCompte, Schensul and Schensul, Mishler, Spradley, Glaser and Strauss, and Lofland. It roughly equates the stages of each with stages in all of the others. The first column represents a synthesis of the scheme used by LeCompte to organize this book (Column 1). Column 2 displays the schema used to organize and analyze quantitative data (domains, factors, subfactors, and variables) described by Schensul, Schensul, and LeCompte in Book 2 and in Chapter 8 of this book.

It is important for researchers to realize that all of these schemes are compatible and can be used together in a study. They simply represent different ways of cutting up, dissecting, and rendering manageable the complex stream of behavior that ethnographers try to understand. We suggest that readers may want to refer to the original sourcebooks in which these strategies are described for more details about their use. In the next chapter, we describe how codes arrived at either inductively or deductively are applied to data and subsequently enumerated.

TABLE 5.1 Comparison of Inductive Analytic Strategies

LeCompte	Schensul and Schensul	Mishler	Spradley	Glaser and Strauss	Lofland
1. Item-level analysis: Identifies items or units; create taxonomies (classify and order items or units)	1. Variable definition: Items are identified and organized into variables; organization of items is hierarchical	1. Constructs a chronological narrative: Identifies all narrative clauses or units that cannot be moved elsewhere without change; 2. Categorizes the narrative clauses as a. Abstract or summary b. Orientations of place, time, person c. Complicating actions or what happened d. Results or solution e. Coda or returns to present f. Evaluation of how the speaker felt	1. Descriptive analysis: Identifies items and units from stream and name them; items into categories 2. Groups items into categories and taxonomies	1. Separates discrete items 2. Chunks units or items into catgories	1a. Identifies acts 1b. Identifies activities and settings
2. Pattern level of analysis: Establishes linkages among taxonomies or classifications	2a. Define factors: Organizes groups of variables or taxonomies into domains 2b. Define subfactors: Organizes groups of variables into larger taxonomic units that can then be grouped into domains	3. Identifies the "moves" (interactions that alter or threaten to alter the position or interactants) 4a. Analyzes text (the content domain; tell what the function of each category is) 4b. Finds the coherence relations (the ideational domain or meaning of the story) Local coherence, global coherence, or thematic coherence	3. Creates linkages and identify	3. Aggregates categories into structures or factors	2. Locates patterns of participation

3. Structural level of analysis: also referred to as interpretive or constitutive level of analysis; organizes relationships among patterns into structures	3. Define domains and relationships among domains: Organizes factors and subfactors into larger sociocultural or ecological units	5. Develop themes (recurrent assumptions, beliefs, goals, values, worldview cognitive map)	4. Develop theoretical constructs	4. Link categories, structures, or factors into theoretical constructs	3. Link patterns into relationships and structures
4. Interpretation: Provides the meaning of structures in relation to existing or new theoretical frameworks and paradigms	4. Interpretation: interprets the relationships among domains via factors (blocks of variables) and individual variables in relation to existing or new theoretical frameworks and paradigms	6. Interpretation: Interprets meaning of themes	5. Interpretation: Identifies meaning of theoretical constructs	5. Interpretation: Develops or selects theories to assist in explanation of theoretical constructs	4. Interpretation of meanings assigned by participants to relationships and structures

6

CREATING A CODEBOOK

WHAT IS A CODEBOOK?

Once the ethnographer has worked through one—or several—of the inductive procedures described in this chapter, he or she will be ready to begin systematically reading through and coding data. There are a number of tasks that must be done to facilitate this process, the most important of which is to create a **codebook**. Codebooks are created once a coding system has been devised and more or less finalized—and we must emphasize that in ethnography, analytic tasks almost never are completely finished and etched in stone! Codebooks always include a complete list of

Definition:
A codebook is a list of all of the codes used for the analysis of a particular collection of data, the names of the variables that the codes represent, and a list of the kinds of items that are to be coded for each variable

- All of the options available for each code (for closed-ended questions or scales), or
- A substantial number of examples illustrating the kinds of units—behaviors, actions, beliefs, ideas, people, events, activities, and so on—for which the coder should be looking when he or she is searching for items upon which to use each particular code, or
- A set of criteria spelling out which characteristics should be present in a unit before it is coded with that particular code

The excerpt in Figure 6.2 is from a codebook that was developed for an instrument that used both closed-ended

VARIABLE NAME	QUESTIONS
ILKETEAC	Do you like your teachers?
NOTLIKE	What don't you like about your teachers?
BORING	What makes a teacher boring?
INTEREST	What makes a class interesting?
PROBLEMS	Have you had any problems with your teachers?
WHATPROB	What problems have you had with your teachers?
THREAT	Have you ever been threatened by a teacher?
PHYSTHRE	Have you ever been physically threatened by a teacher?
EMOTHRE	Have you ever been emotionally threatened by a teacher?
CLASSEAS	Do you think your classes are easy?
EASCLASS	Which of your classes is the easiest?

Figure 6.1. Variable names and associated questions for the Black Knight High School student survey codebook.

questions (such as the precoded questions about gender, age, and number of "no grades" or failing marks a student received in the previous semester) and open-ended questions with short answers to assess the feelings that American Indian high school students had about school. The researchers first created variable names for each open-ended question, as indicated in Figure 6.1. Each of these variable names was limited to eight characters, given the specifications of the software (SPSS, the *Statistical Package for the Social Sciences*) used to analyze these data. For example, one of the questions was, "How many 'NG' grades did you receive last semester?" The variable name was "NUMBNG," which does not make much sense unless the reader or researcher knows that "NG" stood for "No Grade," an evaluation that was given to students who, despite their poor or even failing performance, were pitied by their teacher. Students in the high school, however, called them "Navajo Grades," noting that white students never received them. An appendix to the general codebook should tell the reader which specific questions on the survey instrument are associated with which variable name, as well as provide explanatory information such as the above, so that years later, or in the hands of another researcher who did not collect the original data, the information would still make sense.

Next, the researchers listed the codes for the closed-ended (precoded) questions. They then did a content analysis to determine appropriate categories and associated codes for the answers to the open-ended questions, and added them to the codebook (see Figure 6.2). Coders coded information from the completed survey instruments onto coding sheets first, after which the lead researcher recoded a sample of the surveys to check on the accuracy of the coding. Once the accuracy check was done, the data were entered into a computer for tallying and statistical analysis.

Cross Reference: See Book 2 for a discussion of content analysis of texts and documents

Codebooks are important even if the researcher is counting tallies by hand. Too many researchers have piles of old data, all well-coded but undecipherable because the researcher cannot remember what the codes stand for and has lost the all-important key: the codebook.

Ethnographers who are using computers for their data entry and manipulations—and most ethnographers now use computers for virtually all but the most simple of studies—should decide on the software they will use and learn its characteristics and requirements first—before they create the codebook. This is because different software packages require different setups and different kinds of input. Regardless of the software used, the codebooks for instruments such as surveys, standardized interviews, and questionnaires should be ordered more or less according to the question order on the instrument. When the codebook is constructed, it is a good idea to leave space here and there for the addition of variables and codes, just in case the process of analysis generates new options that the researcher feels are important to consider.

Column	Variable Name	Question#	Codes
1-3	ID#		enter number
4	Gender	1	1=male, 2=female
5-6	Grade	2	enter number
7-8	Yeargrad	3	enter number
9-10	Age	4	enter age
11	NumbNG	5	enter number
12	Help	6	1=yes; 2=no; 0=blank
13	Liketeac	7	1=yes; 2=no2; 0=blank
14-15	Notlike	8	01=talk too much
			02=disorganized
			03=unavailable
			04=don't listen, don't care
			05=poor appearance
			06=too easy, no challenge
			07=unfair
			08=other
			09=unfriendly, don't joke
			10=complain too much
			11=negative attitude toward students
			12=uninterpretable
			13=too much work for time
			14=teachers are good
			00=blank, no answer
16-17	Boring	9	01=talk too much
			02=teach something we already had
			03=teach a boring subject
			04=when they don't get kids involved in class
			05=when they do nothing
			06=when they talk about themselves
			07=don't put in effort to teach
			08=other
			09=too rigid, strict, no time to relax
			10=when they are absent
			11=when students misbehave
			12=uninterpretable
			00=blank, no answer
18-19	Interest	10	01=involves kids in class
			02=lots of activities
			03=well-organized
			04=interesting subject; activities
			05=helps students, is understanding
			06=allows games, play, makeup time
			07=positive attitude
			08=other
			09=teacher likes students
			10=uninterpretable
			00=blank, no answer
20	Problems	11	1=yes; 2=no; 0=blank

Figure 6.2. Codebook for the Black Knight High School student survey, Fall 1991.

Column	Variable Name	Question#	Codes
21	Whatprob	12	1=I don't have problems 2=teachers lie 3=they are naive, innocent 4=insult students; are unpleasant, jerks 5=they ignore students; don't care 6=flirting; sexual advances with female students 7=physical contact; hit, grabbed, shook a student 8=other 9=give you time out 0=no answer, blank
22	Threat	13	1=yes; 2=no; 0=blank
23	Physthre	14	1=yes; 2=no; 0=blank
24	Emothre	15	1=yes; 2=no; 0=blank
25	Classeas	16	1=yes; 2=no; 0=blank
26-27	Easclass	17	01=all 02=reading 03=English 04=mathematics 05=band 06=U.S. studies 07=Spanish 08=other 09=vocational education 10=Seminary 11=state studies 12=art 13=P.E. 14=none 15=science

Figure 6.2. Continued

We think it is a good idea to code all numerical data—or data whose codes are numeric—on coding sheets before they are entered into a computer. In fact, many surveys are pre-coded and the survey responses are coded by the interviewer or the respondent of the survey is self-administered. It is usually a good idea not to do direct entry from the instruments or field data themselves, because mistakes in coding are more difficult to locate. The coding sheets also can be a valuable backup if disks or data tapes are destroyed or lost, so they should be saved with the codebook and other valuable data, in copies kept separate from each other. Ethnographers should verify a sample of both the coding and the data entry for accuracy before continuing with data manipulations.

USING A COMPUTER FOR CODING OF TEXT DATA

Computers have made the lives of ethnographers immeasurably easier and often cheaper. In the following box, we list some of the principal ways in which computers can assist in the organization and analysis of text data.

> *Analytic Tasks That Computers*
> *Can Perform for Researchers*
>
> - Produce copies of raw data
> - Collate or partition data files or documents
> - Store head notes, memos, and researcher musings in a separate document
> - Search for words or phrases in interviews, fieldnotes, and other data documents and retrieve text portions that include those words or phrases
> - Attach identification labels to prestructured units of text, such as responses to a questionnaire, and then sort the data by each label
> - Divide data into researcher-determined or naturally occurring language analysis units, such as sentences or paragraphs
> - Help in preliminary coding prior to the creation of a more refined classification system
> - Sort, collate, and print out coded data segments (or units of analysis) into preliminary categories to facilitate their comparison and refinement into a more developed classificatory scheme
> - Insert researcher-developed codes into data files or memos as the researcher reads through data
> - Enter final codes into data, and then sort, assemble, and print out data segments (or units of analysis) according to the researcher's categories
> - Count the frequency of coded segments or units in each category
> - Identify coded data segments as relevant to two or more categories, which helps researchers to discover linkages and associations between and among coding categories

- Count the frequency of co-occurrence of segments or units in two or more categories
- Retrieve coded data segments or units from subsets of data—females only, for example—in preparation for contrasting them with other subsets
- Search for and identify segments in the data that appear in a certain sequence—such as chronological sequence
- Search for groups of related codes within data files in preparation for exploring linkages among the categories
- Create graphic displays of hierarchical or temporal relationships between and among categories of data
- Transfer data segments in the form of quotations into research reports (Tesch, 1993, pp. 280-281)

Users of computer programs for the analysis of text data need to decide whether it is worthwhile to use a computer program for the management of text data, and which kind of program they will find most useful. Four important decisions are the following:

- How much data are likely to be collected. It is probably not worthwhile to use a computer to code fewer than 100 pages of text data because of the time required to code it.
- Whether codes can be entered directly into the text, or whether the text will be coded later. Entering codes directly into the text so that they can be found later using search commands requires that the coding system be fully developed in advance. Entering the codes later provides the lattitude for allowing the final coding system to evolve from the data.
- Whether qualitative and quantitative data should be integrated in the same data set. Some software programs, such as NUD·IST, allow researchers to integrate SPSS files with text files and convert numerical coding of text data to SPSS files. For researchers who are interested in collecting different kinds of data on the same topic, these programs can be very helpful.
- Whether audiovisual data will be incorporated into the data set and coded. Until recently, it was not possible to combine

audio and visual data with text data in desktop or laptop computer hardware-software configurations. Now, new programs enable researchers to code audio and video data on the screen and to search text, audio, and video databases simultaneously for coded segments. Like text-only computer software, they organize the segments into a single file that researchers can then scan, organize, analyze, and interpret.

It is important for novice ethnographers to remember that computers alone do not analyze or even code data. They are designed only to help to expedite these operations when researchers are working with large bodies of text and other kinds of data. The process of coding, retrieving, and subsequently mulling over and making sense of data remains a laborious process *completely controlled* by researchers. Even if a computer is used, researchers still must go through the process of punching each code into the data on the computer as they read through their interviews, fieldnotes, audio-, and videotapes. Computers are merely handy and extremely fast labeling and retrieval tools. Researchers also must remember that they alone can tell or program the computer to retrieve and count data in specific ways; the machines do not do it automatically. Fortunately, a number of computer programs now exist that make this process relatively straightforward—always, of course, under the direction of the researcher! One early discussion of such computer programs can be found in Renata Tesch's chapter in LeCompte and Preissle's (1993) text, *Ethnography and Qualitative Design in Educational Research.* A thorough review of computer programs for analysis of qualitative data as well as good suggestions for ways of proceeding with data analysis can be found in Weitzman and Miles's (1994) publication titled *Computer Programs for Qualitative Data Analysis.*

SUMMARY

In this chapter, we have discussed how researchers use coding systems to create and differentiate the taxonomies and categories of items they have identified in their data, as well as to count the number of such items in each category. Such a process, whether it yields actual frequency counts or is limited to more subjective creation of relative weights, helps to establish the variance within the cultural scene under study. This process is critical to outlining the complete cultural portrait that is the ultimate goal of an ethnographer's work. In the next chapter, we talk about how coded data are assembled to create cultural patterns and structures.

7

PRELIMINARY RESULTS: IDENTIFYING PATTERNS AND STRUCTURES

Up until now, we have talked about relatively concrete items or units that are relatively easy to identify and well differentiated from each other. Many of these items are like the descriptive codes we defined earlier; they have clear boundaries and are the easiest to find, code, and enumerate. However, other important kinds of data are more elusive—that is, they illustrate phenomena that are hard to operationalize except in terms of multiple discrete behaviors (see the example of "respect for elders" in Chapter 4) that do not have clean beginnings and endings, and that may have multiple meanings. They include such things as meanings, motives, themes, explanations, causal links, complex activities or belief structures, patterns of interaction, practices, or norms and values. Often, these must be identified in terms of some cover term or category name that stands for a complex of behaviors or ideas, as is the case of "Intensity" in the Arts Focus Study (see Figure 7.1) or "Respect" in the Learning Circle study (see Example 1.1).

Cross Reference: Book 2 discusses the importance of initial modeling in framing data collection and the initial organization of data in the analysis phase

The identification of items often is guided by a preliminary model stemming from the study's research questions or concerns. This preliminary model, which usually includes an initial set of items, patterns, and even guesses about structures, is elaborated and refined as data are collected and organized during the study, new items are identified, and items expected to be present are not found and thus eliminated from the model. LeCompte's initial coding system (discussed in Example 2.7), which she developed in her pilot study, was elaborated in this way in the light of further information that emerged as she completed the fieldwork in her actual research. An excerpt from these coding categories was presented in Figure 4.2. Similarly, the formative theoretical frameworks developed by Schensul and colleagues in their studies of young women and sexual risk in Mauritius were transformed into initial coding taxonomies and refined and expanded as data from different sources were accumulated.

Cross Reference: See Chapter 4, Figure 4.4, in this book

A Note on When to Code

Some methodologists argue that data should be coded as soon as they are collected; Miles and Huberman (1984) even say, "Don't go to bed until the day's fieldnotes are coded." However, as you can see from the descriptions of the various forms of coding discussed above, that admonition applies only to those situations in which the fieldworker has done considerable research prior to entering the field; already knows what things are important to notice and what those things look like in the field; is knowledgeable about where in the field these things are to be found; and has a protocol or list of codes already established to use on the fieldnotes or observations. Angela Smith's research on humor (see Example 4.3) is such a study; although she coded directly from observation, she also could have written down her observations in the form of fieldnotes first and then coded them. Incidentally, doing so would have preserved more of the context in which humor events were used, and that could have permitted explorations of how, under what conditions, and with whom graduate students used humor, rather than simple frequency counts of types of humor use alone.

We generally suggest that ethnographers should not engage in rigorous and specific coding unless and until they have done enough fieldwork to be able to develop codes that meet all of the requirements spelled out in the above pages. Premature coding is like premature closure; it can prevent the investigator from being open to new ideas, alternative ways of thinking about a phenomenon, and divergent—and sometimes quite correct—explanations for events. It could be argued that Angela Smith prematurely closed off her coding procedures and, in this way, limited what she might have learned about the use of humor not only in graduate school, but also as a tension-reducing strategy in a number of stressful situations. Many computerized text data management programs, such as NUD·IST (1995), permit the development of free nodes, which are emergent coding categories that are not yet assigned to a location in the coding tree or taxonomy. They allow ethnographers to identify and assign new codes while continuing to refine the definition of the coding category. When the concept is fully operationalized, the code is assigned to its permanent position in the coding tree.

As we have discussed, analysis is a kind of playing with ideas; part of the usefulness of the play is its creativity and flexibility. Ethnographers should not stop playing the game before it is over!

THE PATTERN LEVEL OF ANALYSIS

Once data are coded, researchers can begin to examine collections of codes to see how they are related to each other.

We call this stage the pattern level of analysis. Pattern-level analysis involves organizing related items (or indicators of a variable) into higher-order patterns (which we call sub-factors in the schema presented in the next chapter). Eventually, patterns are organized into structures (which we call factors) and, finally, linked to theories from various paradigms that help to explain their existence.

The pattern level of analysis is something like the middle stages of assembling a jigsaw puzzle; once the player has found all of the orange pieces and all of the blue pieces, for example, or all of the pieces with a particular pattern on them, he or she then can begin to assemble those pieces into a coherent chunk of the design portrayed in the completed puzzle. Furthermore, the player can begin to see how the orange chunks are related to the blue chunks, or where they fit into the overall picture. Ethnographers sometimes talk rather intuitively about how patterns emerge from the data; although the process *does* involve a bit of intuitive thinking, there are, in fact, some rather systematic ways of looking at data that facilitate the process.

HOW DO PATTERNS EMERGE?

Patterns emerge in ways that can include the following:

- Declaration
- Frequency
- Omission
- Similarity
- Co-occurrence
- Corroboration
- Sequence
- A priori hypothesizing

We now discuss in more detail what researchers do when they are using the above strategies to identify patterns in their data.

Patterns Emerge by Declaration

Sometimes, informants will tell a researcher that a pattern exists; in those cases, researchers can look for data that confirm or deny the informant's declaration. For example, in Jean Schensul's study of hard drug use among teens and young adults, a key informant told a member of the research team that he preferred to continue his association with street life while also working in a regular job, so that he could "keep his feet in both worlds." The pattern of maintaining connections in two or more sectors emerged early in the study and constituted a focal point for further exploration.

Patterns Emerge Because of the Frequency With Which They Occur

One very common way to identify patterns is in terms of the frequency with which specific items, events, responses, kinds of person, or themes occur. When a particular unit, theme, or idea appears over and over in the data, then researchers can feel fairly certain that a pattern may exist. A case in point is LeCompte's repeated observation that some or all of the four behaviors (units) that illustrated parents' involvement in Learning Circle schools (Example 1.1 in Chapter 1 of this book) were frequently linked. She eventually decided that, taken together, they constituted a pattern that she referred to as "Respect."

Patterns Appear Because of Omission

Another common, but often overlooked, form of pattern is one identified in terms of something notably *missing*. For example, despite the fact that women and men in the field of public education attain the same amount of education and training, men still dominate all forms of leadership in schools, and women are almost totally absent from the ranks of large city school superintendents. Or, in a study exploring supports and barriers to asthma compliance in young children, omission became apparent when researchers sought but did not find community-based informational resources on asthma management for families.

EXAMPLE 7.1   ━●━●━●

PATTERNS IDENTIFIED THROUGH OMISSION: NOTICING GAPS IN SPECIAL
EDUCATION INFRASTRUCTURE IN A SUBURBAN ELEMENTARY SCHOOL

In a study of parental involvement in placement decisions for children with special needs, one important first step was to identify the places (i.e., meetings and other settings) where informal as well as formal decision making regarding special education placement took place. The second was to study the roles of the various participants in this decision-making process. The third was to consider the facilitators and barriers to parental participation in the process. During the second stage of the study, researchers Schensul and Robertson noticed that parents who were well informed and outspoken came to both child study team and pupil placement team meetings, and those who remained relatively silent came only to the child study team meetings. With further probing, Schensul and Robertson discovered that the more frequent attenders lived in the "hills" outside the town in the wealthy suburbs, and those who came only the first time or not at all lived in the "flats" near the school. They attributed this pattern to social class differences (Pelto, Schensul, & Yoshida, 1978).

━●━●━━

Patterns Appear Because of Similarity

Items, events, responses, people, or themes often appear to clump together because they are similar to one another. LeCompte and Holloway first noticed that the theater teacher in the Arts Focus program frequently addressed the students as if they were already actors (e.g., "Now, this line is supposed to be funny. You all are actors; you know how to put humor across."). Later, they noticed that not only did she use a variety of other ways to refer to students as actors, but that all four of the Arts Focus teachers referred to their students as if they were artists. For example:

- "Now, composers always sign the music they write. So put your name at the bottom of your score."
- "Artists always keep their brushes clean. Make sure that yours are washed out before you leave."
- "Let's brainstorm some ways to get the work of all you writers published."

Frequency counts first identified the pattern of address in the theater teacher's class; the existence of similarity then established a pattern of alternative ways to address students as artists in her classroom and in those of the other teachers as well.

Patterns Emerge Because of Co-Occurrence

Patterns also can be identified by the fact that items, events, responses, kinds of people, or themes occur at the same time or in the same place, that is, they appear to be correlated. LeCompte and Dworkin (1991), for example, noticed that schools where teachers had high levels of burnout and feelings of entrapment also had higher percentages of students who dropped out of school.

PATTERNS IDENTIFIED THROUGH CO-OCCURRENCE: ASSOCIATIONS
BETWEEN AGE AND USE OF HIGH-RISK, DRUG-USING SITES

In a study designed to determine whether it would be useful to locate HIV prevention activities in urban sites where drug users were injecting drugs and sharing needles, researcher Kim Radda identified a range of sites from outside, public, and exposed, to inside private apartments or behind locked doors of public bathrooms. She then asked whether different types of people might prefer one kind of site over another. Based on observations and preliminary ethnographic survey data, the first choice for most drug users consisted of public sites, which were less safe but easier to access. Older drug users also selected outside public locations as their first choice but did so in smaller numbers. Their second choice was the apartment of someone they knew, and a much larger percentage of older than younger drug users made this choice. Radda theorized that the discomforts of using drugs outside coupled with the fear of being caught by the police prompted older drug users to look for safer and more private locations, even if they had to reduce the frequency of their drug use (Radda, Schensul, Clair, & Weeks, 1998).

➤•➤•➤

Patterns emerge as one piece of data is corroborated by others.

The process of triangulation often can unearth patterns as responses, items, events, or themes from various sources of data begin to corroborate one another.

EXAMPLE 7.3

PATTERNS IDENTIFIED VIA TRIANGULATION AND CORROBORATION

Medina discovered a pattern of social class differentiation among Navajo teachers and teacher aides when she compared fieldnote data from three different settings: a camping trip on a remote mesa at the end of the school year for elementary school children, their teachers, and the teachers' classroom aides; in classrooms; and in meetings of the bilingual program's staff. Medina noticed that teachers asked aides to do all kinds of menial tasks and felt uncomfortable when aides demonstrated knowledge superior to theirs in some specific areas. For example, on the camping trip, some of the teachers came dressed in the same good clothes they wore to work, systematically requested the aides to prepare and serve coffee to them, and left the job of sleeping in the tents with children to the aides, while they slept in their nearby campers and recreational vehicles. In the classrooms, aides usually were asked to work with the most difficult and least able students—those to whom was attached the least social status. And in the bilingual meetings, teachers were uncomfortable when it became obvious that they sometimes had to rely on aides who, despite their lower status, sometimes were more fluent in Navajo than the teachers themselves. Medina reasoned that the teachers, with their college degrees, felt that they had attained a status level higher than that of the aides, who sometimes had less than a 2-year Associate of Arts degree. Teachers seemed to feel the aides needed to "pay dues" by performing less pleasant tasks—as the teachers themselves felt they had done earlier in their careers (Medina, 1998).

Patterns Appear as Sequences

Patterns also appear as a sequence, usually temporal, of items or events. Rituals and repeated practices often show up as an invariable sequence of behaviors, as Holley and Doss (1983) found when they noticed that—contrary to common belief among teachers and school administrators—young women who became pregnant did not drop out of school when they got pregnant or when their pregnancies became noticeable, or even when the babies were born. Rather, the sequence that predicted dropping out of school was the following: *First,* the young women gave birth. Next, the young mothers' child care arrangements failed, and only *then* did they drop out of school. Dropping out, then, was a child care issue, not one of motherhood alone. Dropouts stayed home because they had to care for their babies.

Patterns Appear in Congruence With Prior Hypotheses

Even before their actual fieldwork begins, researchers may sometimes hypothesize that patterns exist. Based on their prior experience, readings, and the theories that informed their work, they decide in advance that a specific pattern *should* exist, and they look for confirmatory or disconfirmatory evidence. LeCompte proceeded in this fashion to look for a pattern of teacher behavior that encouraged student achievement *for its own sake,* thus supporting the intrinsic value of learning. This pattern, however, was found in the behavior of only one of the four teachers in the Learning to Work study. LeCompte and Holloway hypothesized that arts instruction *should* involve a variety of strategies for inducing students to think in imaginative ways; they structured both their observations and their data analysis so as to identify this kind of instruction. Similarly, Schensul, Schensul, and Oodit hypothesized that there would be significant differences in risk behaviors between urban lower-income and university youth, and, because of the emphasis on maintaining female virginity, gender would play an important role overall and within these sociogeographic groupings. Both semistructured and ethnographic survey questions were formulated to test this hypothesis. Data analysis using both sources of data confirmed the predicted differences among groups in attitudes toward sex and drug-related risk behaviors, with urban young men most likely to engage in smoking, drinking, and risky sexual behaviors, followed by university males, urban women, and finally, female university students (Silva et al., 1997).

Patterns can emerge as the study progresses, becoming more and more elaborated throughout its life. New sub-components of the patterns can emerge at any time during the study, and these can be added to guide further data collection and analysis. The major domains or cultural components of interest in the emerging patterns then become the initial categories for organizing and coding. This was the case in the Arts Focus Study, whose analytic framework is described below and displayed in part in Figure 7.1. In this case, the researchers began with some initial hunches and ideas about the impact of arts education on students that were based on their reading of research literature and theory prior to beginning the study, as well as their own experiences in music and creative writing. At the end of the first year of observations and interviews, the researchers began a systematic review of their data, looking for themes that seemed to be the most important emphases in the program in terms of what the teachers articulated as goals for their students and what they seemed to stress in their classrooms. LeCompte and Holloway developed a preliminary set of domains with subdomains and concrete examples of what kinds of behavior each subdomain represented. Some of the domains and subdomains came from the theorists they had read; these are indicated in parentheses in Figure 7.1. The rest emerged from the data in a laborious process of reading and rereading the fieldnotes, transcripts of interviews from students and teachers, and documents from the program. The result, an excerpt of which is displayed in Figure 7.1 (pp. 106-111), was an initial analytic scheme for the data. Figure 7.1 also includes a number of

Cross Reference: See Book 3, Chapter 1, and Book 2, Chapters 2 and 3, for a discussion of cultural domains

(text continues on page 112)

DOMAIN	SUBDOMAIN: WHAT TEACHERS DO	EXAMPLE	SUBDOMAIN: WHAT STUDENTS DO	EXAMPLE
Embodying or being an artist	Provide role models who are professional artists	• Visits to artists' workplaces, studios, backstage, foundry, book fairs • Guest artists and writers	• Watch artists at work • Study lives and works of practicing artists • Visit artists' workplaces	
	Teach professional demeanor and decorum	• VA: Sign a painting in cursive [To the class] "Remember how we sign it in cursive" • TA: Maurita demands quiet backstage because it is heard by the audience	• Model artists' demeanor	
Referring to students as artists, actors, musicians, and writers	• TA: "You [students] are actors; you know how to put over a line" • IM: "As a composer, you always put your name on your piece"	• Presenting self as artist		
Acquiring an artists' tools, skills, and practices	Teach concepts (vocabulary, registers, and genres) of specific arts disciplines	• VA: "Lots of people think abstract art and non-representational art are the same thing, but they're not" • VA: "Pop art is about shape" • VA: "I want you to understand these terms: realism [explains], photorealism [explains], abstract, and nonrepresentational"	• Emit and use the language of artists	

Identify, procure, and use tools that artists need for practice	• TA: "We're going to have a make-up man come in, and the first thing he'll tell you is to have your own makeup kit. For $30, you can get a start-up kit"	• Assemble a toolkit
Teach professional secrets, tricks, and tips	• TA: "No jewelry. It reflects on stage" • LA: On why author wrote biography as a novel: "I think it was a publisher's decision. They probably thought kids wouldn't buy an autobiography" • VA: "Wash your brushes or they'll get hard and useless"	• Translate experience into imagery, sound, movement, and characterization
Identify sources of inspiration and mentors	• Art teachers all tell stories about who and what inspired them and from whom they learned	• Seek and identify mentors and sources of inspiration

(continued)

DOMAIN	SUBDOMAIN: WHAT TEACHERS DO	EXAMPLE	SUBDOMAIN: WHAT STUDENTS DO	EXAMPLE
Disciplined creativity	Teach how to stimulate creativity to get started	• LA & IM: Encouraging students to come up with new ideas for compositions and interpretations of pieces • VA: Teacher to student who cannot figure out what to do with his painting: "Remember your resources. Go to the books. Look at other landscapes. That's what resources are for—either you can come up with ideas on your own or you have to use resources to help you get ideas." • VA: Viewing multiple versions of "Romeo and Juliet" and reading the play before designing sets • LA: Using previous pieces or others' writing to generate new ideas for pieces	• Describe their own strategies for generating creativity	

Teach how to get unstuck once started	• VA: Showing students how to gain perspective by putting work up and stepping back from it • LA: Teacher instructing to start in the middle of a work if one cannot get started at the beginning and to read other works within the same genre • TA: Teaching stage-fright exercises	• Demonstrate strategies for getting unstuck	• LA: Jena creating a book of prewriting exercises and activities • VA: Students putting their work up on a wall and getting others to consult on it
Internalize or "fossilize" the rigors of everyday practice (Vygotsky)	• TA: Teacher, "Diction is something you work on all your life. If you have braces, it's harder" • TA: Warm-ups every day, rehearsals • LA: Multiple drafts; writing every day • VA: Multiple sketches • IM: Multiple drafts of compositions and rehearsals; practicing every day	• Choose to practice skills outside of regularly scheduled classes	
Risk taking	Solicit criticism or feedback	• LA: Teacher asks students to write letters telling him how they feel about his leaving for New Zealand at semester's end	• Defend one's own opinions or actions • Offer one's own work for critique • Offer critique to others

(continued)

109

DOMAIN	SUBDOMAIN: WHAT TEACHERS DO	EXAMPLE	SUBDOMAIN: WHAT STUDENTS DO	EXAMPLE
	Publicly confront controversial or delicate subjects	• VA: Teacher takes students on field trip to university where they will see full-frontal male nudity • Social studies teachers invite a Socialist Worker party candidate to address their class	• Take stands on public controversies	
	Perform	• VA: Teacher learns piano and talks about her first recital • TA: Assistant principal plays part of Prince in "Romeo and Juliet"	• Take part in public performance • Assume nontraditional roles	• LA: Public readings at town Bookstore and Arts Center • TA: Girls playing male characters • TA: Students taking roles as leaders and directors
Decision making	Identify problems	• LA: On teacher's blackboard: "What *didn't* go well?" • TA: After exhibitions: "Why wasn't it successful?"	• Engage in brainstorming sessions in class and in small groups	
	Teach strategies for breaking down a project into stages		• Identify the steps for accomplishing a project	
	Solicit the opinions and participation of others	• LA: "I would like to see how you feel about meeting here [in library]. I would love to have you where there are books"	• Ask others to participate in a project	
	Deliberate, think things through, and plan	• LA: Teacher, "What would we like to do next?"	• Think through and plan a project	• TA: Small groups discuss and write out short scenes on index cards before practicing

	Choose a course of action	• Decide on a course of action	• VA: Teacher, "If you want it to look this way, you could leave it alone, unless you like it better the other way"	• TA: Small groups practice invented scenes
	Debrieing: critique both the execution of a project and the work itself	• Engage in debriefing		• TA: Small groups stop and discuss their scenes as they practice, afterwards noting changes on their cards or script
	Revise based on lessons learned	• Revise or producing multiple versions of projects		• TA: Students develop multiple versions of their invented scenes before presenting them to class and public
Intensity	Encourage focus, convergent thinking, concentration	• Exhibit ability to focus on activity • Get into character	• TA: Teacher on scene of T.S. Eliot's "Cats": "Don't listen to the poem. Be cats!"	
	Provide commitment of resources: time, materials, and emotions	• Spend more time than is minimally needed to get the job done • Buy or procuring one's own supplies or resources • Talk about one's emotional investment in an activity		
	Emphasize hard work	• Working through difficult problems and activities • Taking on tasks that are more difficult than required		

Figure 7.1. Teacher domains from the Arts Focus program.

the specific behaviors and statements from teachers and students that exemplify what the researchers meant by the specific cover terms they used. Blanks in Figure 7.1 indicate that specific behavioral indicators for that domain still need to be isolated from the data. Note that "IM" stands for "instrumental music," "TA" for "theater arts," "VA" for "visual arts," and "LA" for "literary arts"; the other initials stand for specific teachers.

This scheme was used in two ways: First, to code data already collected, such as fieldnotes and interview transcripts; and second, as a focus for subsequent observations in classrooms. At the end of the second year of fieldwork, it also was used to classify information about the responses or reactions of the students to what the teachers were doing and information about what the students said they were getting out of the program.

LeCompte and Holloway also found that they needed to add subdomains and items to the original existing domain categories—including some of those developed in the Learning to Work study. These, in turn, were used as codes for data that were then classified and manipulated. The process described here is parallel to the development of formative theory, or theorizing, as we describe it in Book 2 and earlier in this book. As we said earlier, theorizing occurs throughout the life of an ethnographic study, and it is only at the end that the study's explanatory model is fully developed.

Cross Reference: See Book 2, Chapters 2 and 3, on formative theory

SUMMARY

In this chapter, we have discussed the way ethnographers use coded data to identify the patterns and structures that constitute the cultural portrait they are trying to assemble. In the next two chapters, we describe how this process works for the organization, management, and analysis of ethnographic survey data.

8

MANAGING QUANTITATIVE DATA

Up to this point, we have been discussing generic ways of organizing and managing text data. In this chapter and the next, we will review the primary ways of organizing, managing, and analyzing quantitative data collecting through ethnographic surveying. Ethnographically informed surveys (cf. Trotter & Schensul, 1998) resemble other surveys with several significant exceptions:

Cross Reference: See Book 2, Chapter 8, on structured data collection and ethnographic surveys

- They are based, at least to some extent, on a locally derived theoretical model (i.e., local theories) that may or may not be linked to more general theories of behavior and culture.

- Scale items are derived from prior ethnographic research that has identified which domains, factors, variables, and items are locally significant and important to the study.

- They are usually (although not always) administered face to face.

- The survey questions interface naturally with coded text data because the coding system used to organize text data originates with the topic of the study, on one hand, and the primary domains structuring the questionnaire on the other.

- They are not likely to include a large number of nationally validated scales or other measures; those that are chosen for inclusion are likely to have been tested with similar populations and locally validated.

These characteristics have implications for the way survey data are analyzed and integrated with other types of data in an ethnographic study.

RETURNING TO THEORY

Definition: A variable is a characteristic, descriptor, or idea that is possessed by the units in a study population in differing or varying degree

Cross Reference: See Book 2 and this volume, Chapters 4, 5, 6, and 7

Variables are the building blocks of ethnographic and other surveys. In Table 8.1, we revisit the framework presented in Book 2 that illustrates where variables fit in the organization of both qualitative and quantitative schema. Variables are at the lower end of the continuum, and the items of which they are composed approximate or act as proxies for observed or understood local facts. In the approach we present in Book 2 and in this volume, exploratory and semistructured data collection methods provide the background material that enriches our formative theory and begins to illustrate issues related to our research questions. These methods also provide the data from which items used to construct survey variables can be culled.

Variables are measured by descriptors, elements, or facts that indicate whether the variable is present or not (qualitative), and to what degree (quantitative). For example, the variable "intimacy with one's adult parents" can be measured by the presence or absence of elements, items, or descriptors such as "writing letters to parents," "visiting parents," "calling parents on the telephone weekly," "living near one's parents," and "living in the same house as one's parents." In ethnography, as we have said elsewhere, we conceptualize variables in both terms. Both qualitative and quantitative data analysis proceed by building up from items and variables (units) to factors (patterns), domains (structures), and paradigms as follows:

Cross Reference: See Book 1, Chapter 2, for a discussion of units of analysis

■ Units—*variable level.* Units can range from simple alternate attributes (e.g., yes/no responses) to more complicated sets of attributes (rankings or combinations of items)

TABLE 8.1 Linking Theoretical and Operational Levels in Ethnographic Research

	Structure	Pattern	Unit	Fact
Domain	Family dynamics and Life achievement			
Factor		Parental discipline and Job performance		
Variable			Modes of parental punishment and Ability to supervise employees	
Item				Frequency of spanking and Frequency of evaluative feedback to employees

■ Patterns—*subfactor and factor level.* Patterns are relationships among variables measured or assessed either qualitatively or quantitatively.

■ Structures—*domain level.* Structures are relationships among patterns (consisting of clusters of variables).

In Table 8.1, we illustrate these relationships.

In Chapters 4, 5, and 6 of this book, we discussed how we qualitatively construct variables (units) out of items. In the next section, we describe how we construct variables—the basic building blocks of theoretical or explanatory development, as well as of survey construction and analysis—in quantitative terms.

Structuring or Building Variables

Survey questions and quantitative data analysis use one of four different types of variables. In quantitative research, these are referred to as *measures* because they measure

Cross Reference: This section should be read in conjunction with Book 2, Chapter 8, on survey construction

variation in the variable in terms of numbers. The kinds of measures are

- Nominal (categorical)
- Ordinal
- Interval
- Ratio

 Definition: Nominal measures are variables whose attributes differ in terms of quality but not quantity

Nominal measures. **Nominal measures** are variables whose attributes are exhaustive (i.e., complete) and mutually exclusive (i.e., there is no overlap of meaning or definition among items or attributes that compose the measure). Nominal measures do not vary in terms of amount, only in terms of quality. We can say that they are categorically different; that is, they can be differentiated by name or label only, not by quantity. For example, in an international training program that brings together people from different countries, people could be grouped by country. The variable would be "country of origin." All people from Zimbabwe, Ireland, Peru, and Indonesia would differ by one characteristic: country of origin. All those from Zimbabwe would share the same characteristic "Zimbabwe as country of origin." People can be arranged in the same way by gender (male vs. female), food preference (vegetarian vs. nonvegetarian), home tenancy (home ownership vs. rental) or meeting attendance (present vs. absent). But the differences between these attributes cannot be ranked. They are simply categorically or qualitatively different. The following are examples of questions based on categorical variables:

Do you belong to a church?   Yes ___   No ___

Are you: Female ___   Male ___

Choose the after-school activity on which you spend the most time
___ Sports ___ Clubs ___ School newspaper ___ Hanging out

Are drugs sold in your neighborhood? Yes ___   No ___

Do you have a boyfriend/girlfriend?   Yes ___   No ___

Ordinal measures. Variables with attributes that can be said to have "more or less" of something are referred to as **ordinal measures.** When we say that attributes have "more or less" of something, we mean that the differences are relative to or ranked against one another but not measured in absolute terms. For example, we can say that teachers can be "more or less" satisfied with a new curriculum but the units or degrees of satisfaction are qualitative. The specific amount of satisfaction cannot actually be measured in degrees of equal weight. The so-called distances between levels do not have any meaning other than "more or less than," especially because the way in which individuals interpret categories may differ. Each of the responses, a - e, taken from a curriculum satisfaction survey used with teachers to assess receptivity to a new social development and AIDS curriculum, is an ordinal variable.

Definition: Ordinal measures have attributes

My students have done very well in mastering:

(Please circle your answer to each one of these skill areas)

	Strongly Disagree	*Disagree*	*Agree*	*Strongly Agree*
a. impulse control	SD	D	A	SA
b. anger management	SD	D	A	SA
c. empathy	SD	D	A	SA
d. problem solving	SD	D	A	SA
e. AIDS knowledge	SD	D	A	SA

Likert scales which ask respondents to rank a preference or opinion from 1 to 5, are ordinal measures.[1] Examples of questions based on ordinal variables are the following:

- How often have you seen freaky dancing in music videos?

  ___ Never ___ Rarely ___ Often ___ Always
- How widespread do you think verbal harassment is in your workplace?

  ___ Very widespread   ___ Somewhat widespread

  ___ Not very widespread ___ Not at all widespread

■ Rank from 1 (*highest*) to 6 (*lowest*) the importance of the
following reasons for dropping out of school

___ Taking care of a baby

___ Working to support a child

___ Getting lazy (feeling tired during pregnancy or after birth)

___ Low self-esteem

___ Poor grades

___ Working to support your household
(parents, brothers and sisters, or other relatives)

Interval measures. Interval measures are defined as variables in which the distance between attributes has meaning as measured with a standard unit of measurement but the base is not zero. It is difficult to find variables in social science research that are true interval measures that are not based on a zero start point. Some authors give the example of IQ or other intelligence scores in which the distance between a score of 100 and 120 is considered to be the same as the distance between 90 and 110, but for a living person, the start point could not be zero—that is, no living person could be considered to have no intelligence functions at all. Even if he or she were brain dead, the presence of some bodily functions would indicate intelligence, even if it could not be measured. An example of a question based on an interval measure is, "How much do you weigh?" No respondent would ever answer "nothing" to this question.

Ratio measures. Ratio measures are based on a true zero point. Actual age, absolute income in monetary units, numbers of people in personal networks, or spatial units such as miles or kilometers are ratio measures. Questions reflecting a ratio measure are the following:

■ How old are you now? Years ___ Months ___

■ What is your estimated monthly income from all sources?

■ How many people live on this block?

Question formats should reflect these measures, and researchers should be clear about why question formats are chosen and generally how they are going to be used in data analysis. This is important because different procedures are used to explore the range of variation in each of these measures and to establish relationships among measures of the same and different types.

ORGANIZING ETHNOGRAPHIC SURVEY DATA

Organizing ethnographic survey data for analysis calls for selecting computer analysis software, establishing a process of entering data, naming and defining variables, making sure that the entry process is quality controlled, and **cleaning the data** to prepare for data analysis.

Definition: Cleaning data refers to making sure that data have been entered correctly, as well as repairing data entry errors

Selecting Data Entry and Analysis Hardware and Software

A calculator and a pad of columnar or ledger sheets might be good resources when researchers need to conduct analyses rapidly and, as often happens, are far from computing resources. Nowadays, however, we recommend that all quantitative data be analyzed by computer. Many software packages exist to help new and experienced data analysts. The most popular desktop software packages are SAS and SPSS; both are sold on the basis of **site licensing.** EpiInfo, a data analysis software package developed in association with the World Health Organization, is used by epidemiologists and researchers in other disciplines, especially in the developing world. It can be downloaded and is available free of charge. There are also simple data analysis packages that new users and teenagers or younger children can use. Many nonprofit organizations prefer to use SPSS (*Statistical Package for the Social Sciences*) for desktop com-

Definition: Site licensing refers to the purchase of a software program for desktop computer use at an initial cost per person and an annual registration fee

puters because it is readily accessible, menu driven, and less expensive than SAS.

A statistical software package allows researchers to enter data or import it from other data management programs such as Excel or Access, perform transformations on variables, use a variety of different statistical procedures, demonstrate results in different visual formats, and prepare and print reports. Graphic results from the two packages mentioned above can be transported into word processing software such as Word and WordPerfect, or directly into presentation software such as PowerPoint or Corel Presentations.

Electronic data can now be tailored for use with ethnographic survey data by using electronic data entry hardware and software. However, high-powered desktop computers with good memory and storage capacity, a high-resolution scanner, and software for creating data entry forms specific to each study's survey instrument are needed for such purposes. Data are collected and coded using these forms. When scanned, the data on the forms are entered directly into statistical software databases, which must be conceptualized and prepared in advance. An example of such a form is presented in Figure 8.1.

Hardware and software for desktop electronic data entry currently are still quite expensive, although they are priced to be purchased by university departments and centers and larger nonprofit organizations. It takes some time to create data entry forms that can be scanned and read accurately into data analysis software. Once the form is created, however, the entry process is swift and efficient. Those who once entered data by hand can then spend their valuable time correcting any entry errors and cleaning data. The microcomputer electronic data entry market is still in its infancy, but it has high appeal for ethnographers who are conducting surveys with large sample sizes (more than 400 persons) because it is efficient and accurate.

Master ID# ☐☐☐

	SITE 1	SITE 2

Q42. What drugs have you used or seen being used at this site?
(Interviewer: Do **NOT** read list; code **first 3** responses)   43A. ☐☐   ☐☐

1 = Heroin	6 = Alcohol
2 = Cocaine	7 = Marijuana
3 = Crack	8 = Everything
4 = Speedball	9 = Other
5 = Methamphetamine	–8 = Refused

43B. ☐☐   ☐☐

43C. ☐☐   ☐☐

Q43. How were those drugs being used?   44A. ☐☐   ☐☐
(Interviewer: Do **NOT** read list; code **first 2** responses)

1 = Injected	4 = Swallowed
2 = Smoked	5 = All ways
3 = Sniffed	–8 = Refused

44B. ☐☐   ☐☐

         N Y DK   N Y DK

Q44. Are needles available at this site than can be used to shoot up
(not brought by you)?   ☐☐☐   ☐☐☐
(Interviewer: If "crack only" site, skip to Q50. If "NO," go to Q45.
Q44a. (If Yes to Q44): Are these needles new, used or both?   ☐☐   ☐☐
     1 = New   2 = Used   3 = Both   –7 = DK   –8 = Refused

         N Y DK   N Y DK

Q44b. (If Yes to Q44): Is there a charge for needles at this site?   ☐☐☐   ☐☐☐

Q45. Have you seen Hartford NEP needles being used at this site?   ☐☐☐   ☐☐☐

Q46. Are clean cookers and cotton available at this site
(not brought by you)?   ☐☐☐   ☐☐☐

Q47. Is unused bleach that you did not bring with you available
at this site?   ☐☐☐   ☐☐☐
Q47a. Have you seen people use bleach to clean their needles
     at this site?   ☐☐☐   ☐☐☐

Q48. Is clean water available at this site (not brought by you)?   ☐☐☐   ☐☐☐

Q49. Is there anybody at this site who would stop or prevent sharing
of needles or other equipment?   ☐☐☐   ☐☐☐

Q50. Are crack pipes available at this site (not brought by you)?   ☐☐☐   ☐☐☐

Q51. Have you seen people having sex at this site?   ☐☐☐   ☐☐☐

Q52. Have you seen people exchanging sex or drugs or cash here?   ☐☐☐   ☐☐☐

Q53. Are condoms available at this site (not brought in by you)?   ☐☐☐   ☐☐☐

         N Y Ref   N Y Ref

Q54. In the last 7 days, have you had any kind of sex with anyone
at this site?   ☐☐☐   ☐☐☐
Q54a. (If Yes to Q54): In the last 7 days, how many times have
     you had any kind of sex at this site?
       (–6 = NA   –7 = DK   –8 = Refused)   ☐☐   ☐☐

Q54b. (If Q54a is 1 or more): In the last 7 days, how many
     times have you had any kind of sex without condoms
     at this site?   ☐☐   ☐☐

Q55. In the last 7 days, how many times have you used drugs at this site?   ☐☐   ☐☐
(Interviewer: After completing Q55 for Site 1, return to Q36b and
complete Q37-Q55 for Site 2)

Figure 8.1. Electronic data entry form, used with an interview.

Developing a Coding
System for Data Entry

Electronic data entry requires the creation of a coding system along with the survey instrument because data are scanned directly from the instrument into a database. However, not all surveys are precoded. Novice researchers, in particular, usually create surveys without defining and naming variables for analysis in advance. In so doing, they create for themselves a very big job later, once their surveys are administered and collected.

The first step in organizing ethnographic survey data is the development of a coding system that establishes and defines the basic set of variables that constitutes the database. The best way to create a codebook is to envision it as the questionnaire is being constructed. The coding system generally follows the questionnaire sequence. It is important to remember that questions in a questionnaire do not always translate directly into single variables. Some questions may include multiple variables, such as when they are composed of a list of "yes/no" responses or a set of Likert scales. In such instances, each response is represented by a separate variable in the codebook.

Steps in developing a codebook are similar to those listed for qualitative data in Chapter 6.

Naming the variable. Software requirements limit the number of letters in a variable to 8. For example, HHAGE = Age of household head; SPAGE = age of spouse; LOCRESID = Location of residence; ATTAIDS = Attitudes toward AIDS,

 Key point   and so on. *Because of time constraints, some researchers may be tempted to list variables by number rather than naming them. For new researchers, this makes learning and remembering the variables much more difficult.*

Describing the variable. To describe the variable, it is necessary to know how the variable is to be represented. Important elements in the description are whether the variable is

■ Numerical
■ A date
■ A currency unit
■ Alphanumeric (letters/words)

The width of the numerical variable (how many spaces it occupies) and whether it includes a decimal point also are important. These decisions are embodied in the codebook formats and instructions. The computer software chosen will determine these and other characteristics of the variable, and it will provide space for entering them and part of the variable's definition. The same software will usually generate a printed version of the codebook based on the data entry system, once it is in place.

Labeling the variables. Labeling describes the variable and labels the attributes or items that characterize it. Most software packages do not require the labeling of variables in order to perform analyses. However, it is always best to insert them in the definition of the variable because they are printed with the output. This makes reading the output much easier.

Variable and value labels should be clear. Examples of nominal, ordinal, interval, and ratio measures (or variables) are illustrated in Table 8.2. As new variables are created and added to the database, they should be added to the codebook as well as defined in the software database.

Constructing New Variables

Except in the case of standardized instruments, researchers rarely work just with the variables that represent

TABLE 8.2 Examples of Variable Names, Labels, and Values for Nominal, Ordinal, Interval, and Ratio Measures

		Nominal Measures
Variable Name	Variable Label	Value Label
BPLACE	Place of birth	1 = San Juan
		2 = Caguas
		3 = Ponce
		4 = Mayaguez
		5 = Other city
DROPED	Main reason for dropping out of school	1 = Pregnant/baby
		2 = Work to support family
		3 = Work to support self
		4 = Bad grades
		5 = Family problems
An example of an ordinal-level variable:		
EDLEVEL	Ed. level completed	1 = Elementary/middle
		2 = High school or equivalent
		3 = Some college/technical
		4 = Completed college
		5 = Postgraduate
		8 = Not relevant
		9 = Don't know
An example of an interval-level variable:		
SATSCOR1	First SAT score	Actual score (No student would receive a 0)
An example of a ratio-level variable:		
HHAGE	Age of household head	Actual age in years (0-100)

each of the items on the ethnographic survey. Instead, the analyst is constantly transforming these variables for purposes of data reduction, analysis, and more effective representation. The following example illustrates how new variables can be created from existing ones.

EXAMPLE 8.1 ━━●━◆━●━◆━

TRANSFORMING ONE VARIABLE INTO ANOTHER THROUGH RECODING

Table 8.3, titled "Age Range in a Youth Group," illustrates the age range in a youth program of the Institute for Community Research.

This table produces a curve skewed toward older youth, as illustrated in Figure 8.2.

TABLE 8.3 Age Range in a Youth Group

		Frequency	Percentage	Valid Percentage	Cumulative Percentage
Valid	13	8	10.4	10.4	10.4
	14	2	2.6	2.6	13.0
	15	5	6.5	6.5	19.5
	16	8	10.4	10.4	29.9
	17	4	5.2	5.2	35.1
	18	22	28.6	28.6	63.6
	19	16	20.8	20.8	84.4
	20	12	15.6	16.0	100.0
	Total	77	100.0	100.0	100.0

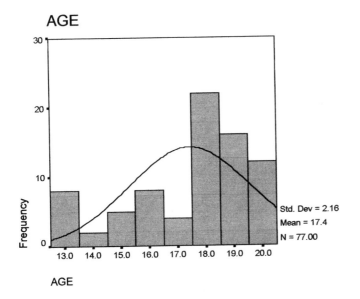

Figure 8.2. A skewed frequency distribution.

For some analyses, it may be better to reconstruct age as a nominal variable, recoded into two categories. Table 8.4, titled "AGECAT," recodes age into two categories, "17 or below" (.00) and "18 or above" (1.00).

The histogram in Table 8.4 is more "normal"—that is, the distribution of the two categories is roughly equal, as illustrated in Figure 8.3.

TABLE 8.4 "AGECAT"

		Frequency	Percentage	Valid Percentage	Cumulative Percentage
Valid	.00 17 or below	27	35.1	35.1	35.1
	1.00 18 or above	50	64.9	64.9	100.0
	Total	77	100.0	100.0	

AGECAT

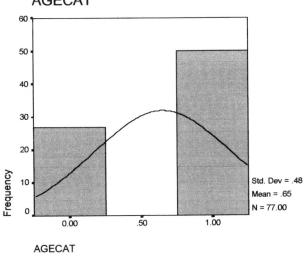

Std. Dev = .48
Mean = .65
N = 77.00

AGECAT

Figure 8.3. AGE recoded into AGECAT, a categorical variable showing a more normal distribution.

Other reasons for the creation of new variables include the following:

- The creation of scales and indexes; for example, counting correct answers to AIDS knowledge questions
- Clustering variables (see section on factor analysis below)
- Combining two variables to create a new variable; for example, subtracting "respondent's ideal age at first sex" from "reported age at first sex," yielding a new variable called "discordance between real versus ideal age at first sex"

Another interesting example of this sort that demonstrates the utility of combining two or more variables into a third comes from data on young women in the Mauritian workforce. The procedure involved subtracting the number of years worked in the industrial sector from the age of the respondent, yielding the new variable "age of entering the industrial workforce." By creating this new variable, we were able to discover that 13% of the sample had entered the workforce prior to 15 years of age, the legal age for entry into the workforce.

We estimate that in a typical ethnographic survey data set, every variable in the original data set eventually will be transformed into a new variable for analysis. It is important to label and define new categories and keep comprehensive notes on the construction of the new variables. If this is not done, the database will become clogged with a number of potentially useful variables rendered useless because no one can remember how they were constructed or defined.

Developing the Structure for a Quantitative Database

Quantitative databases are basically of two types:

- Simple databases, sometimes called "flat files," consist of a matrix of "cases" along the side (people or other units) and variables along the top. Most of the databases created by ethnographers who are working with **cross-sectional** survey data will be of this type.

- Relational databases consist of multiple databases linked to each other by a common identifier. This allows different levels, or types, of data to be kept and analyzed separately. Sections of each data set consisting of groupings of variables can be selected later, along with the unique identifier, and joined with each other to form new databases. Longitudinal studies, which collect the same data at two points in time, often are kept in this way. Items to be compared from each data set are then combined later on, using the unique identifier.

Definition: Cross-sectional refers to data collected at only one point in time

🐷 **Cross Reference:** See Book 4, Chapter 1, on types of network data and examples of data collection matrices

Network data can also be kept in this way. Network research calls for collecting information about the individuals in one person's network. Network data sets often are very large. When demographic, household, and psychosocial data are collected on an individual, as well as network data, a flat file could be enormous and time-consuming to manage. Thus, it is efficient to organize the network data collected from each individual in the study into a separate file. This allows the network data to be analyzed separately, consolidated, or crunched, and then linked to the index person's demographic/household database.

It is important to make decisions as to which type of database will be needed for a study early in the process of conceptualizing the database because the decision will affect how many sub or smaller related databases are established, through what mechanisms they should be related, and what software will be most useful in establishing and connecting them. For anything more than a flat file, a relational database management system, such as Access, is much more efficient because it allows data from two or more linked data sets to be extracted and merged much more easily. We refer readers to the manual for the *Statistical Package for the Social Sciences* for more information on conceptualizing and constructing databases.

Entering Data

🐷 **Cross Reference:** See Book 6, Chapter 2, on data entry and management in multiple sites

Depending on the scope of the project, size of data entry staff, and time constraints, data can be entered by the research staff or by employees of data entry firms. Survey data can be keyed in by hand or read electronically. In studies carried out across sites, data are usually entered in one location and shared with other sites. Table 8.5 lists some examples of projects in which data were entered in a central location and shared.

TABLE 8.5 Cooperative Studies With Shared Data Entry Procedures

Study	Location	Types of Data	Data Entry Arrangements
National Institute of Drug Abuse: NIDA Cooperative Agreement (number) (six sites)	Flagstaff Hartford New York Puerto Rico, etc.	Quantitative, drug-related AIDS risk behaviors	—Data entered at each site —Site data sent to a central location and entered by hand —Integrated data sets shared with all sites
Center for Substance Abuse Prevention: CSAP Cross-Site Youth at Risk study (144 sites)	One to six sites in every state	Standardized Behavioral Risk Survey Instrument	—Data collected locally and sent to central location —Data entered by hand centrally and clean data sets sent to local sites for review and use —Amalgamated data set used centrally for cross-site analysis
Institute for Community Research and University of Illinois: AIDS and Aging study (two sites)	Two cities	Standardized AIDS and drug risk behavioral and network survey instrument	—Data entered electronically at both sites —Data consolidated at one site and shared with both sites —Single-site and cross-site analysis
Hartford AIDS Research Consortium Institute for Community Research and Hispanic Health Council (one site, eight projects)	One city, same site	Similar instruments with specialized components specific to each project	—Project data entered electronically —Data shared with participating consortium members

Once the data entry process is organized, the data manager must then

- Review the completed instrument to make sure that the instrument is complete, the data are coded correctly, and there are no missing data
- Send instruments back for review and completion if they are incomplete
- Make copies of all completed instruments prior to data entry, because accidents can happen and data can be lost
- Arrange for data to be entered; if data are entered by hand, rather than electronically, they should be double entered or checked to ensure accuracy

■ Run frequencies on all data regularly as the data are being entered to make sure that there are no inappropriate entries (entries outside the appropriate numerical range) and to assess how much missing data there might be

As we have noted, using an electronic data entry system requires setting up electronic data entry forms. These forms follow the format and content of the questionnaire, providing boxes for data codes. Some scanning programs read numbers only; others have the capacity to read script. It is important to train those who are collecting data using electronic forms very well so they record their data carefully in ways that scanners can read their entries accurately.

Once data are entered, several backup copies of the original data set should be made and kept in a separate location, preferably locked for safety reasons. Nothing is worse than losing a data set. Raw data should always be stored and kept until a study has come to an official end. Some researchers follow the 7-year rule, keeping their raw data stored for that length of time before destroying it.

Data Cleaning: Tidying Up

Tidying up quantitative/survey data prior to data analysis involves producing frequencies to make sure that data are entered accurately and there are no unusual **outliers.** For example, entries of 4, 5, and 7 would be outliers for the variable "sex," in which 1 = male and 2 = female, and any other option would not make sense. Where there are unexpected numbers, or where the distribution of a variable does not look right (e.g., does not fit, is skewed or biased in an unexpected direction), it is important to return to the data entry screens to see whether there are mistakes in entry or, if necessary, to return to the original questionnaires. Computerized and electronic data entry systems help to save

 Definition: A quantitative outlier is an entry that is less than or more than the proper range for that variable

time at this stage because they set limits to the range of numbers that can be entered for any given variable. Thus, it is impossible to enter a code that does not fall into the range of acceptable responses for variables.

DATA MANAGEMENT

Frequencies

Once data are cleaned, the first step in data management is to produce **frequency distributions**. For the purpose of identifying problems with individual cases or the data set, frequency distributions should be produced regularly during the time the data are being entered.

As we have discussed in other books in this series, ethnographic surveys are based on both random and systematic sampling procedures. Outliers can be eliminated from the variable descriptors by recoding them as missing data or "other"; or the variable can be redefined to incorporate the outlier in some reasonable manner. For example, in a data set on injection drug users, two individuals who self-reported as injecting more than 250 times a month were viewed as outliers and removed. Furthermore, the questionnaires for these cases were reviewed to see whether they produced outliers on other variables. If a case demonstrates a number of outliers, the data may be incorrectly reported or recorded; alternatively, the case may be unusual, warranting a review of the original data and treatment as a example of an extreme case. It is also possible to adjust for outliers by normalizing a distribution through log transformations. (Figure 8.4 illustrates a normal curve.)

The production of a non-normal curve in a randomly sampled population may have to do with the characteristics of that population (e.g., what kind of adolescents were included, and excluded, from the population). Once the

Definition:
A frequency distribution shows the number and percentage of cases responding to each of the attributes or descriptors for a variable, and the number of cases that are missing a response for that variable

Cross Reference:
See Book 1, Chapter 5, on research design and on units of analysis and sampling, and Book 2, Chapter 9, on random and systematic sampling

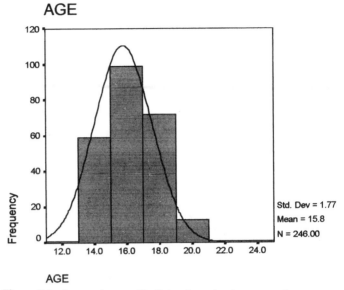

AGE

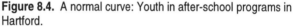
AGE

Figure 8.4. A normal curve: Youth in after-school programs in Hartford.

 Definition: Parametric statistics are those procedures that can be used to show relationships among variables in a random sample, whereas nonparametric statistics can be used with nonrandom samples

reasons for the skewing have been discovered, decisions must be made regarding whether **parametric** or **nonparametric statistics** should be used for analytical purposes. Parametric statistics require impeccably drawn random samples, which, as we note in Book 2, are difficult to create in many field situations because the requirements for constructing them appropriately, including normal distribution of characteristics within the population, cannot be met. With nonrandom samples, however, nonparametric statistics can be used. Nonparametric statistical techniques parallel parametric statistical techniques; they permit researchers to consider relationships among variables in nonrandomly selected samples. We will explain this distinction further in the final section of this chapter and refer readers to introductory statistics texts for more advanced discussion of these issues.

Consolidating Quantitative Data
(Data Reduction or Crunching)

Ethnographers tend to collect large amounts of survey data because they are interested in seeing the ways in which many social, cultural, or environmental factors influence individual behavior or beliefs. This produces a large number of variables. Ethnographers are not unique in this preference, however. Multivariable epidemiological surveys, panel studies, national surveys, and cross-site studies with many cases often produce very large data sets.

Just as we consolidate or crunch text data to reduce pages of fieldnotes to a manageable number of concepts, we can also engage in reduction of quantitative data into a more manageable data set that may show relationships more clearly. There are several common procedures for consolidating quantitative data. All of them are ways of combining several related indicators into a composite variable.

Indexes and Scales

Indexes and scales are similar to one another in that they rank order people or other units into a sequence with respect to the selected variable. For example, a Material Infrastructure scale that includes seven items (rent/own home, mud/cinderblock walls, thatched/tin roof, plot/no plot, presence/absence of electricity, presence/absence of piped running water, presence/absence of inside bathroom) yields a score of 0 to 6. Those whose score is 0 have none of these items; those whose score is 6 have all of them.

As composite variables, indexes and scales can often provide a better or broader range of variation than a single variable. Furthermore, indexes can sometimes give a better or more comprehensive indication of a variable than a single item. The Material Infrastructure items listed above, when added together, give a better indication of material

wealth than, say, rental or home ownership alone. There are
four principal kinds of scales used in social science research:

- Index construction
- Scale construction
- Guttman scaling
- Factor analysis

 Definition:
An index is
created by
summing the scores
of two or more
variables in a set

Index construction. An **index** is constructed simply by adding up scores assigned to attributes or indicators in a related
set of variables into a total score. The index range is from
the lowest to highest possible score. Each attribute in an
index has equal weight in relation to the others. To construct
an index from the items in the Material Infrastructure listing above, an ethnographer would assign 1 to the presence
of each item and add the total. Table 8.6 displays an index
for Material Style of Life.

Indexes can also be composed of summed Likert scales.
Likert scales range from 3 to 5 points. All of the subscales
or items in an index composed of summed Likert scales
should have the same number of points (3, 4, or 5 points).
An index composed of five related 3-point Likert scales
would have a range of scores from 3 to 15. Indexes are used
more frequently than scales because they are easier to construct from the available data. But the construction of a good
index is not always easy. The most important things to keep
in mind when constructing an index are the following:

- The items in an index must have face or logical validity. They
  must logically be indicators of the concept indicated by the
  variable. The indicators in the Material Style of Life index are
  material items. Although these material items are probably
  purchased with cash, cash income is not an indicator of material style of life because this scale concerns material items, not
  available cash resources.
- The index must be unidimensional. The items in the scale all
  must relate to the same domain. An index of drug use risk

TABLE 8.6 Items in the Material Style of Life Scale for Sri Lanka

Items	Percentage of the Population Possessing Them (N = 615)
Wall clock	94
Electricity	84
Television	83
Sewing machine	74
Bicycle	50
Motorbike	23
Car	14.7
Telephone	8.8

Material Style of Life Scale for Sri Lanka:
Ranking Frequencies (Ranks range from 0-8 items)

Ranking (0-8 items)	Frequency	Percentage	Valid %	Cum. %
0.00	11	1.8	1.8	1.8
1.00	21	3.4	3.4	5.2
2.00	56	9.1	9.1	14.3
3.00	98	15.9	15.9	30.2
4.00	196	31.9	31.9	62.1
5.00	115	18.7	18.7	80.8
6.00	69	11.2	11.2	92.0
7.00	30	4.9	4.9	96.9
8.00	19	3.1	3.1	100.0

NOTE: This scale approximates a bell-shaped curve in which the median, mean, and mode overlap.

behavior, for example, should not include items related to sex risk, even though risky drug use may be associated with risky or unprotected sexual behaviors. The variable should be clearly defined so as to avoid including in the index irrelevant or tangentially associated indicators.

■ The items should demonstrate variability. If everyone answers an item in the same way (either yes or no), there will be no variance, and the item will not add anything to the index. An item can be selected if responses are split equally (50%/50%, or in equal thirds if it is a 3-point Likert scale); or if items differ in amount of variance (some may be split equally, and some unequally).

■ Bivariate and multivariate relationships among items should be established. Items in an index should be associated with one another (using percentages or correlation coefficients), but the

Definition:
Bivariate refers to relating one variable to another in a 2 × 2 table, whereas multivariate refers to relating two or more variables to a third variable

relationship should not be perfect. If there is a perfect relationship between two items, one can assume that both are indicators of the same thing and can stand in for each other in an index. This is important, because redundant items unnecessarily increase survey length, which is undesirable. It is important to examine the relationships among all the items in an index one by one, as well as together, because two items may relate to each other, but one of them may not relate to a third.

Definition:
Missing data refers to missing responses to a question

■ A way must be found to handle **missing data.** Missing data can be handled by either eliminating the case or inserting a value based on judging the general pattern of response for the total sample or the pattern of response for the individual. For example, an individual may check only those items with "yes" responses, leaving some items blank. Researchers could then assume that the blanks really meant "no."

By considering the relationships of the responses "don't know" to "no" or "yes," with other variables, it may be possible to impute or attribute a value to "don't know." For example, if both relate in the same way to two other important variables, they may be considered similar; in such instances, "don't know" can be recoded as "no" for the purposes of further data analysis. Missing data can also be inserted as proportional by assigning the mean or the range of response values at random. The most effective approach is to construct the same index using several strategies to see whether the same correlations can be found with each.

■ The index must be validated. Validating the index can be done by seeking a correlation of each item to the entire index (Cronbach's alpha is a statistic that measures the degree of correlation or association among items in an index or scale), or by seeking a correlation between the index and another external and widely accepted measure of the same variable. For example, one could correlate estimated caloric output based on number and type of activities carried out during the week against an electronic instrument for measuring energy outputs.

Scale construction. Scales are ordinal rankings of cases composed of different items that represent a range of intensities. For example, a scale of acceptance of nontraditional employment (carpentry, electrical wiring, car engine repair, metal work, masonry) for women in Senegal includes the following items:

- Girls in this community can become masons.
- The masonry work of girls is as good as that of men.
- Girls will be hired to do masonry work in this community.
- I would allow my daughter to become a mason.
- I would hire a girl to do masonry work on my house.

Logical sequencing by intensity or weight in an ethnographic survey is based on an understanding of the significance of each of the items in the cultural context of the community or population for which the survey is being designed. Identification of scale items can take place in the survey construction stage, with validation in the data management phase; alternatively, scales can be constructed after the fact from items already included in the survey that logically relate to one another based on the study itself and knowledge of the cultural context in which it is taking place.

EXAMPLE 8.2

BUILDING SCALES FROM SURVEY ITEMS BEFORE AND AFTER DATA COLLECTION

In an ethnographic survey of factors associated with AIDS risk in Sri Lanka, indicators of knowledge of AIDS risk were identified based on previously conducted semistructured ethnographic interviewing. These items were included in the survey under "knowledge of AIDS risk." Scale construction was carried out during the data management period. In the same study, however, a scale of sexual risk behavior was constructed after the fact from items located in several different sections of the survey.

Guttman scaling. Guttman scaling is a useful scaling technique that lends itself readily to ethnographic data. Guttman scaling is based on the idea that items in a set or sequence can be arranged so that the last (the greatest or most intense) predicts the others. In addition, the items accrue in order (of strength, intensity, risk, etc.) so that the last predicts not only all the others but also the *order* in which they accrue. Guttman scales are based on nominal measures (presence/absence; yes/no).

Building a Guttman scale requires that the researcher first identify the items that logically and culturally fit into a single dimension. Items that often scale using the Guttman technique are specific sexual behaviors (from least to most intimate or risky); items reflecting economic status (land, house style, etc.) or material style of life (items purchased with cash income); and community infrastructure (roads, electricity, health and educational resources, etc.). Attitudes also may scale. Babbie (1995), for example, notes that three items indicating support for abortion—if the woman's health is endangered (92%), if the pregnancy is a result of rape (85%), and if the woman is not married (45%)—probably form a Guttman scale.

Guttman scales can be constructed by hand or by using a computer program (e.g., ANTHROPAC or SYSTAT both include Guttman scaling programs). The scale is created by arranging each case in sequenced order of item accrual. The arrangement takes into consideration the likelihood that there will be exceptions to the pattern and looks for the best fit. Items are arranged across the top and cases along the side, and each group constitutes a scale type. The prototype design is shown in Figure 8.5. The strength of the scale is determined by the number of "mistakes," or incorrect predictions in the cases. The percentage of correct predictions

Behaviors (See list below)							Scale Type (%)
1	2	3	4	5	6	7	
X	X	X	X	X	X	X	7 (42.6)
X	X	X	X	X	X		6 (4.6)
X	X	X	X	X			5 (5.9)
X	X	X	X				4 (4.9)
X	X	X					3 (5.9)
X	X						2 (7.2)
X							1 (15.3)
—							0 (14.6)

Behaviors:
1. Sitting close together
2. Holding hands
3. Love talk
4. Putting head on shoulder
5. Kissing
6. Hugging
7. Putting her head in his lap

N = 615 x 18 items, Scale errors = 700, Coefficient of Reproducibility = .937; Coefficient of Scalability = .772, Alpha = .946

Figure 8.5. A Guttman scale: Male-female intimate behaviors, central province, Sri Lanka.

is referred to as the coefficient of reproducibility. It is a ratio, arrived at by placing the number of empirically derived correct responses (checks in the scalogram) over the number of predicted correct responses and dividing the numerator by the denominator.

In Figure 8.5, there are 56 (7 behaviors × 8 groupings of individuals into scale types) possible correct answers. The scalogram is 100% correct. If there were cases in each scale type in which Xs were present or absent where they should not be (and thus, these cases could not be placed in a perfectly predicted logical order), the number of incorrectly placed Xs constitute the errors, which are then subtracted from the total to give the numerator.

The scale types are entered as a new variable. In Figure 8.5, there are eight scale types, representing different steps in the evolution of intimacy between men and women. The variable "male-female intimate behaviors" would be coded from 0 (Scale Type 1) to 8 (Scale Type 7) and treated as a continuous variable in further analyses.

In addition to the fact that Guttman scaling is a useful data reduction technique, its value in ethnographic research lies in two important characteristics:

- Its dependence on categorical data (nominal scales), which are very useful in ethnographic analysis
- The fact that items in a Guttman scaling emerge empirically from field research in the setting; generally, they cannot be transferred from one site or study to another, even though similar cultural domains tend to scale in this manner

Factor analysis. Factor analysis is used to discover patterns among the variations in values of several variables. This generates statistically constructed dimensions or factors that correlate highly with several of the real variables and are independent of one another. The researcher then attributes meaning to the underlying dimension associated with each statistically determined factor. Factor analysis is appropriately used *only* with data from random samples. The following example is adapted from Forslund, 1980 (Babbie, 1995, pp. 428-429).

USING FACTOR ANALYSIS TO IDENTIFY PATTERNS OF
DELINQUENT ACTS AMONG HIGH SCHOOL STUDENTS

Morris Forslund conducted a study of delinquency among high school students in Wyoming. He was interested in using a list of 24 delinquent behaviors, which was included in his questionnaire, to create a typology of delinquency. A factor analysis was conducted with this list; the result was four factors. The first factor included 11 items with highest factor loadings of between .45 and .66, which accounted for 67% of the variance. The 11 items seemed to be related to destruction of property, so Factor 1 was named "property offenses." The second factor included six different items, with highest factor loadings of between .44 and .64, all of which had to do with acts against the norm or disobedience. This factor was called "incorrigibility" and accounted for 13% of the variance. The third factor consisted of five additional items related to drug use, with highest factor loadings ranging from .31 to .75. It was named "drugs/truancy" and accounted for 11% of the variance. The fourth factor, which included only two items related to physical fighting and had .84 and .60 factor loadings, respectively, accounted for only 8% of the variance. Variances added to 100%. He defined these constructed factors with attributed meaning as delinquency profiles.

━●━●━

The advantage of factor analysis is its ability to integrate and crunch a large number of noncategorical items believed to be at least somewhat related, as well as its quality of inductivity, which resembles the cognitive discovery processes that ethnographers use to organize, analyze, and interpret text data. The disadvantages of factor analysis include its inability to predict factor loadings and consequent lack of previously assigned meaning to predicted factors, and high loadings for unrelated items.

SUMMARY

In this chapter, we have reviewed many of the central concepts in the organization and management of ethnographic survey data. In the next chapter, we introduce procedures for analyzing quantitative data and integrating or triangulating results with other data sources in a comprehensive ethnographic study.

NOTE

1. Guttman scales are ordinal scales that demonstrate logical orderly accrual of attributes or items; that is, they demonstrate the presence of a ranking in a set of items that might rank differently in different cultures or with different populations.

9

ANALYZING
ETHNOGRAPHIC
SURVEY DATA

In the previous chapter, we reviewed the steps required to organize and prepare quantitative data for analysis. In this chapter, we will walk readers through the steps in the analysis of quantitative survey data. The quantitative data obtained from structured observations can be treated in the same manner as survey data, so we will not discuss analysis of observational data separately.

Just as we did in Chapter 8, we begin this chapter by returning readers to the original problem or question posed by the researcher, and to the formative theoretical model or theorizing that guided the development of the quantitative survey instrument in the first place. Analysis of survey data proceeds from this model. In the last section of the chapter, we review approaches to analysis of other types of quantitative data, such as elicitation data (i.e., listings and sortings), network data, and sociogeographic mapping.

LOGICAL PROCESSES: RETURNING TO THE SOURCE

In this book, as well as in Books 1 and 5, we have paid close attention to

- Where research questions come from
- How research questions guide the development of research methods
- The importance of formative ethnographic theories and how they are generated
- The scientific importance of linking research questions, theory, and methods to analysis and interpretation

In Book 1, we referred to research design as a road map or blueprint that researchers develop and follow to arrive at a destination. In ethnographic research, the destination we are attempting to reach is an answer to the research questions we have asked in the first place. Analysis of ethnographic survey data, like the analysis of text data, returns us to our original research question. The original question is usually somewhat broad or abstract. "What is the range of variation in the energy outputs of Latino children of preschool and elementary school age?" "How do family, peer, school, community, and media influence adolescents' drug-related behavior?" or "What accounts for the apparent success of the Arts Focus program?" are typical questions that initiate studies. Quantitative data collected with respect to such questions usually are related to some explicitly formulated hypotheses developed on the basis of prior knowledge or exploratory research. These hypotheses are embedded in the questions included in the survey and the ways the responses are formulated and coded. They can be phrased in the following ways:

- "If X, then Y"
- "X will be more likely to be associated with an event, effect, problem, or outcome than Y"
- Y "causes" or predicts X

In Table 9.1, we have provided some examples of statements based on the above logical equations. Although the equations are slightly different, the logical construction of all of the hypotheses is basically the same. Column 1 of the table states the formal hypothesis. The second column translates it into ordinary English as it is likely to emerge at any point during the study. It is easy to see how the hypothesis, when translated into ordinary English, can be used to guide both qualitative and quantitative analysis. The third column provides an initial interpretation of the hypothesis. Only one or two ideas are expressed in this column. When researchers are seeking to identify and interpret results, they must return to the initial explanation for the hypothesis and verify it in both the literature and the text or qualitative data gathered in the study. We will say more about this in the following chapter on interpretation.

The initial formulation of the research question(s) is stated in the form of questions and subquestions related to a problem or conceptual domain. These are the result of description or exploratory research that begins with a question, or with a formative predictive model identifying dependent and independent variable domains and the relationships among them. The first step in both qualitative and quantitative analysis involves describing the domains in this initial research formulation. Once this is done, as is described in Chapter 8, descriptive statistics (e.g., frequencies, means, modes, and medians), which we address in the following pages, can be used to describe the variables in the study.

The second step involves considering the relationship between each of the independent variable domains and the dependent variable domain. This process is described in the section on bivariate analysis. The third step involves considering the relationships among the independent variables in relation to the dependent variable domain, which we term *multivariate analysis*. Because these three steps involve

TABLE 9.1 Ways of Framing Hypothetical Questions Guiding Analysis of Ethnographic Survey Data[a]

Hypothesis	Translation	Possible Explanations
If-then statements		
If formal education is high, *then* employment status will be high	More formal education results in better employment	Formal education results in more skills; formal education results in more contacts necessary to improve potential for employment
If mothers' activity outputs are high, *then* children's activity levels will be high	Mothers who engage in more activities will have children who do the same	Mothers act as role models for children; mothers are the ones who make decisions about whether or not the activity levels of children are high or low
If one or both parents have health problems, *then* young women are more likely to engage in risky behavior	The health problems of parents will contribute to the involvement of daughters in risky behavior	Sick parents create emotional and financial tension in the household, which leads girls to seek relationships outside
If parents are involved in the program, *then* it is more likely to be successful	Parental involvement in a program will contribute to its success	Parental involvement results in more academic and social supports for children; parents involved in program activities will be more invested in children's participation and performance
Statements of association or correlation		
Girls *are more likely* to engage in activities inside the house than are boys	The gender of a child will play an important role in determining the location of the child's activities.	Parents are more protective of girls and do not allow them to play outside unsupervised
Social influences *are more likely* than are psychological characteristics to be associated with adolescent involvement in illegal activities	Social influences are more important than psychological ones in predicting teens' behavior	Older teens and young adults involved in illegal activities will have an important influence on their peers and will socialize them into illegal activity
Causal or predictive statements		
Low self-esteem *predicts* dropping out of school	Low self-esteem is the most important factor in determining whether a student will drop out of school	Students who have low esteem will not do well in their school work and will not seek out help when they need it

Hypothesis	Translation	Possible Explanations
Exposure to media influence *predicts* sex at an early age	Youth who have more exposure to the media (television, movies, music videos) will initiate sex earlier than their peers	Media portray the benefits of sexual engagement without communicating the disadvantages; youth unsupervised at home after school have a lot of time to watch media with their friends
Inability to recognize and report symptoms of diabetes *predicts* late diagnosis and treatment	People who cannot identify symptoms of diabetes and do not have easy access to health care are less likely to report symptoms, be properly diagnosed, and start treatment early	Two of the biggest problems in the management of adult Type II diabetes are lack of knowledge of symptoms and consequent late reporting to health care providers

a. It should be noted that in all correlational analyses, such as those in this table, a third variable may actually explain an apparent relationship beween the first two. A famous, and humorous, example is the alleged relationship that states that as the number of Methodist ministers in an area increases, so also does the number of alcoholics. The third variable related both to the number of ministers and the number of alcoholics is degree of urbanization; both alcoholics and Methodists are more numerous in urban areas!

rather complex processes with which many new researchers will be unfamiliar, our discussion of them in the remainder of this chapter may prove to be somewhat challenging. We have tried to cover quite a bit of statistical and analytical ground in one short chapter, and for this reason, we suggest that readers examine the sourcebooks we have cited in the bibliography for further information. We also urge readers to look at two very useful books: *Research Methods in Anthropology: Qualitative and Quantitative Approaches* (2nd ed.) by H. R. Bernard (1995), and *Statistics: A Spectator Sport* (2nd ed.) by Richard Jaeger (1990).

DESCRIPTIVE STATISTICS

Step 1 in the analysis of ethnographic survey data is to describe each of the variables in a variable domain using descriptive statistics. Descriptive statistics describe

- The distribution of the variable (range of variation)
- Typical value of the variable (mean, median, and mode)
- Variation around the typical value (variance and standard deviation)
- The shape of the distribution (a curve or histogram)

Range of variation is displayed with a frequency table. A frequency table gives the actual numbers and percentages of cases by variable value. The table for each variable will look different, depending on whether the variable is a nominal, ordinal, interval, or ratio measure. Examples 9.1 through 9.4 demonstrate frequencies for each of these different measures.

EXAMPLE 9.1 ━━●━━●━━

RANGE OF VARIATION IN ATTRIBUTES OF THE NOMINAL
VARIABLE GENDER AMONG LATINO ADULTS WITH DIABETES

Variable Value	Count	Cum. Count	Percentage	Cum. %
Female	66	66	66.0	66.0
Male	33	100	33.0	100

EXAMPLE 9.2 ━━●━━●━━

RANGE OF VARIATION IN THE ATTRIBUTES OF THE VARIABLE TITLED HOUSEHOLD
SOCIOECONOMIC STATUS (ORDINAL MEASURE); TOTAL SAMPLE SIZE $N = 130$

Variable Value	Count	Cum. Count	Percentage	Cum. %
Low	27	27	21	21
Medium	67	94	51	72
High	36	130	28	100

EXAMPLE 9.3

RANGE OF VARIATION IN THE ATTRIBUTES OF THE VARIABLE
TITLED SAT "SCORES"[1] (INTERVAL MEASURE); TOTAL SAMPLE SIZE N = 550

Variable Value	Count	Cum. Count	Percentage	Cum. %
900-1000	120	120	21.9	21.9
1001-1100	100	220	18.1	40.0
1101-1200	90	310	16.3	56.3
1201-1300	87	397	15.8	72.1
1301-1400	63	460	11.4	83.5
1401-1500	54	514	9.8	93.3
1501-1600	36	550	6.5	99.8

EXAMPLE 9.4

RANGE OF VARIATION IN THE ATTRIBUTES OF THE VARIABLE TITLED "AGE OF
INITIATION OF ALCOHOL USE" (RATIO MEASURE); TOTAL SAMPLE SIZE N = 120

Variable Value	Count	Cum. Count	Percentage	Cum. %
9 years	12	12	10.0	10.0
10 years	15	27	12.5	22.5
11 years	22	49	18.3	40.8
12 years	31	80	25.8	66.6
13 years	15	95	12.5	79.1
14 years	13	108	10.8	89.9
15 years	12	120	10.0	99.9

The following example shows how frequencies can be used to describe certain characteristics of the family structure of young women respondents in the Mauritius industrial sector.

EXAMPLE 9.5   ◆▪◆▪◆

USING FREQUENCIES TO DESCRIBE THE FAMILY STRUCTURE OF
YOUNG WOMEN IN THE MAURITIUS INDUSTRIAL WORKFORCE

The first step in analysis of the qualitative and quantitative data from the Mauritius study of young women, work, and AIDS was to describe the variables in each of the domains in the original formative theoretical model—family, peer, and work (see Figure 10.8 in Chapter 10 of this book). In the analysis of the ethnographic survey, the following variables were grouped into a factor referred to as "family structure"; it consisted of father's role in the family, mother's role in the family, and sibling structure. Frequencies were obtained for all of these variables and explained with ethnographic text data. Fathers were explored first.

Frequencies included the following:

Presence of Fathers (Total Number = 498)	N (total)	Percentage
Absent	165	33.1
Present	333	66.9

Physical Condition of Fathers (Present in the Household) (Total Number = 333)		
Unhealthy	158	47.4
Healthy	175	52.5

From the frequencies derived from these two categorical or nominal variables, researchers Schensul and Schensul determined the total number of fathers missing or unhealthy to be 323, or 64.9%. The frequencies suggested that in almost two thirds of the households (323), fathers were either missing or physically impaired.

A similar analysis was conducted for mothers and siblings. Mothers were present in 464 (93.2%) of the 498 households from which young women were interviewed. Of these, 219 mothers were working (47.1% of those present), and 158 (31%) reported having health problems. In 60% (296) of households, at least one sibling also was working in the industrial sector.

Because adult men make twice as much money as women, households in which fathers and at least one child are working are likely to be better off than households in which siblings only, or both mother and siblings are working.

We will return to this hypothesis later in this chapter when we discuss the role of bivariate analysis.

Central Tendency

Central tendency is a measure that sums up the variable for the population. There are three measures of central tendency: the mean, the median, and the mode.

Definition: Central tendency is a measure of the typical or general value of a variable

Measures of Central Tendency

- Mode: The mode is the attribute that occurs most often. In Example 9.4, the mode is 12 years of age.
- Median: The median is the midpoint in the scores in a distribution. In Example 9.4, the median is also 12 years of age.
- Mean: The mean is the average of scores for a variable. The mean in Example 9.4 is 12.9.

Example 9.6 shows how means can be used to make sense of research data. This example uses means of ranked data; some statisticians do not recommend calculating means from scaled or ranked data, believing that interval or ratio data are the only acceptable data types from which to calculate means. We include this example because many researchers do, indeed, calculate means from other-than-ratio-and-interval data.

➤•➤•➤   **EXAMPLE 9.6**

MEANS FOR REASONS FOR GOING TO WORK AMONG YOUNG WOMEN IN MAURITIUS

The ethnographic survey used in this study asked 498 women respondents to rank six reasons for going to work that were derived from exploratory and semistructured data collection. The ranked mean scores for each of the reasons are the following:

Reason	Mean Score
To support the family	2.0
Financial independence	2.6
To be away from home	3.2
To avoid boredom	3.7
Friends were working	4.6
Family problems	4.7

Respondents rated each of these reasons against every other. The most important reason for working given by this population of young women was to support the family; the second most important was for financial independence. The mean scores suggest that *most respondents* (central tendency) chose the first two items as either their first or second choices. These two reasons for work are potentially contradictory if the young woman must use most or all of her salary to support the family when, in fact, she anticipated gaining some economic independence from the family. This suggests that many young women may experience considerable conflict both internally and with family members with respect to their work and use of their income.

➖•➖•➖

The above example indicates how means, as one measure of central tendency, can be used to describe an important dimension of a sample, as well as how the data may be discussed and tentatively interpreted at this stage of the analysis.

Measures of central tendency all portray a general picture of the main pattern or trend in the target population. The median is a more stable measure than the mean because the mean can change dramatically with one or two outliers, whereas the median remains approximately the same regardless of outliers. However, if the distribution is symmetrical, that is, it can be portrayed in a normal curve, then the mean is the best measure of central tendency to use. So-called normal distribution means that the distribution of a characteristic is most dense at the median, or midpoint, and progressively—and symmetrically—less dense at each end of the distribution. Such distributions are required in order

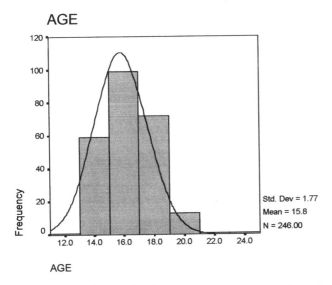

Figure 9.1 A normal curve showing corresponding mean, mode, and median.

to use many kinds of statistical procedures; to the extent that they do not exist in the database, researchers must accommodate their analyses to specific peculiarities of the data. Clearly, having done fieldwork prior to working with quantified data helps researchers understand just why a population's characteristics might not be normally distributed.

Measures of Dispersion

Measures of dispersion provide information on the degree of variation in the sample. They include the variance and standard deviation. Different patterns of dispersion in distribution of data or scores result in different shapes in the distribution curve. A symmetrical distribution of values results in a bell-shaped curve (where the median, mean, and mode coincide with the top of the curve; see Figure 9.1). Asymmetrical distributions may be positively or negatively skewed. A positively skewed distribution results if the mode is located to the left of the median. A negatively skewed distribution results when the mode is located to the right of the median. A bimodal distribution occurs when there are two modes or primary patterns.

Standard Deviation

Standard deviation is a statistic that tells researchers how much the scores in a distribution vary or deviate from the mean score. The amount of deviation from the mean lets you know how homogenous or heterogeneous a population is.

How to Calculate the Standard Deviation

Definition: Variance is the average squared deviation from the mean of the scores for a continuous (ordinal, interval, or ratio) variable

To arrive at the standard deviation, first calculate the **variance.** To calculate the variance for each variable of concern, you must

- Find the mean for the variable
- Subtract each observation or case score from the mean
- Square the difference for each result
- Add all the differences
- Divide the sum by the sample size or the N (see Table 9.2)

Table 9.2 gives an example of calculating the variance for "age of population."

Because standard deviation is a measure of variation in the distribution of scores from the mean score, it is calculated by taking the square root of the variance. To find it, first calculate the variance, and then find the square root of that figure.

BIVARIATE STATISTICS

In the next sections, we describe bivariate and multivariate forms of analysis, which are used to explain as much of the

TABLE 9.2 Finding the Variance for Age of a Population (Total N = 120 cases)

Value	N	%	Difference	Squared
9 years	12	11.9 – 9 = 2.9	2.9 × 12 = 34.8	1,211.04+
10 years	15	11.9 – 10 = 1.9	1.9 × 15 = 28.5	812.25+
11 years	22	11.9 – 11 = 0.9	0.9 × 22 = 19.8	392.04+
12 years	31	11.9 – 12 = –0.1	–0.1 × 31 = 3.1	9.61+
13 years	15	11.9 – 13 = –1.1	–1.1 × 15 = –16.5	272.25+
14 years	13	11.9 – 14 = –2.1	–2.1 × 13 = –27.3	745.29+
15 years	12	11.9 – 15 = –3.1	–3.1 × 12 = –37.2	1,383.84
Total	1,429			4,826.32

Mean (Total/N = 1,429/120) 11.9   Variance (Total/N = 4,826.32/120) 40.21

Formula
1. Subtract each observation or case score from the mean
2. Square the difference for each result
3. Add all of the squared differences
4. Divide the sum by the sample size or the N

variance in a selected variable as possible. We first discuss bivariate statistical analysis.

Frequencies and measures of central tendency and dispersion allow us to describe the characteristics of the overall sample in terms of the primary variables in which we are interested, but we can only speculate as to how variables relate to each other within subfactors, factors, and domains. The purpose of bivariate statistics is to enable us to explore statistically the relationships among the variables and groups of variables that we have proposed in our original theoretical model. These statistics help us determine whether these relationships truly exist or are simply random or chance occurrences. Most ethnographically informed surveys contain many variables. For this reason, analysis theoretically could go on forever. Thus, it is important to work with a conceptual roadmap or puzzle design to eliminate guesswork and what are often called planless "fishing expeditions" into the data.

For guidance, we return to our formative theoretical framework. By this time, we should have reduced the number of variables with which we are working by using some of the data-crunching strategies outlined in Chapter 8. And we now have additional hunches based on the emergence of patterns from frequencies and means. Furthermore, we have already begun to fill in the pieces of our puzzle by defining and characterizing the domains in our study's model. If the study is primarily descriptive or inductive, we have, by this time, defined our domains of primary interest and identified other domains that are linked to our central domain in logical ways. If our model is already developed, we have measured in our survey the main variables included in dependent and independent domains. With text and quantitative data (frequencies and means), we have also begun to fill in a more elaborated description of each of the domains in our model. Now our task is to explore (a) the relationships among the main variables in each domain, and (b) the associations between selected independent and dependent variables.

Some researchers argue that life is so complex that we should turn directly to considering the interaction of many variables. Although this may be the most sophisticated statistical approach, we believe that it is better to use our accumulated understanding of the study situation to examine, one by one, the relationships among variables that we think might be most important.

Thus, we suggest that the next step in data analysis should be to examine the relationships among pairs of variables. Bivariate statistics are used to find, describe, and test the significance of the association between two variables. Bivariate associations can be explored with directionality, using Pearson's r correlation, or without directionality, using most other statistics of association. Exploring associations permits us to know

- How strong the association or covariation is
- Whether the association is due simply to chance or whether something specific (i.e., something we recognize in our study or program intervention) is causing it in our sample

- If the association is positive or negative
- Whether the shape is linear or nonlinear

An association between two variables can have

- No relationship (there is no direction to the relationship between income and educational level)
- A positive linear relationship (one variable predicts another in the same direction, e.g., the lower the educational level of respondents, the lower their income level will be)
- A negative linear relationship (one variable predicts another in the opposite direction, e.g., the higher the income the lower the education level)
- A nonlinear relationship (the direction changes at a specific point for predictable reasons, e.g., the higher the income level, the higher the education level—until income reaches a certain point, at which education level begins to drop because inheritance or general business skill supercedes education level in relation to generation of income)

The most frequently used measures of association are chi-square or Fisher's exact test for small cell size (for nominal-level data), gamma or Kendall's tau (for ordinal data), and Spearman's rank order correlation and Pearson's *r* correlation for interval and ratio data unless the relationship is nonlinear. Bernard (1995) suggests using a statistic called eta when the relationship is nonlinear or for establishing relationships between interval/ratio (e.g., age) and nominal (e.g., gender, yes/no) data. Eta enables researchers to separate interval data into nominal groupings, which are then correlated with a nominal measure.

T-test. **T-tests** are tests of association based on comparisons of means. In a study of drug and AIDS risk among youth in Hartford, researchers hypothesized that males would consume more alcohol than females, and that Latino and white youth would consume more alcohol than African American youth. A *t*-test was used to determine whether

Definition:
The *t*-test compares two means to determine whether they are statistically different enough to show actual differences between two populations

there was a significant difference in *amount of alcohol* (a continous variable, measured by number of drinks consumed in the past 30 days) used by girls versus boys, and whether there were ethnic differences in quantity of consumption.

Pair-wise difference *t*-tests are used to test the difference in means between related populations (e.g., using a pair— or pre- and posttest—of means obtained from the same target group of students). For example, in an intervention study at the Institute for Community Research that was designed to prevent risk behaviors in female preadolescents by improving communication between mothers and daughters, a *t*-test was used with a matched sample to determine whether improvements had actually occurred from baseline assessment to immediately postintervention as measured by a self-report communications scale (Romero & Berg, 1998). In a similar assessment of the results of a risk prevention intervention with youth in Sri Lanka, the *t*-test was used to determine whether participants' knowledge of sexual risk prevention as measured by an AIDS prevention knowledge scale (an interval measure) improved subsequent to the intervention (Nastasi et al., 1998-1999).

Analysis of variance (ANOVA). Another statistic that is based on comparison of means is **analysis of variance, or ANOVA.** One-way ANOVA explores the effect of one categorical independent variable (such as sex) on a continuous dependent variable (such as income or attitudes toward school). Two-way ANOVA explores the effect of two categorical independent variables on a continuous dependent variable. The following example shows how one-way ANOVA can be used to display statistically significant gender differences in friendship patterns among youth in Sri Lanka.

 Definition: ANOVA is a statistic that is used to determine whether differences in the means of two or more populations are statistically significant; that is, not due to chance alone

USING ONE-WAY ANOVA TO ANALYZE GENDER DIFFERENCE IN FRIENDSHIP PATTERNS IN SRI LANKA

In a study of youth and AIDS risk in the central province of Sri Lanka, a total sample of 615 young people were interviewed. Approximately half were drawn from an urban low-income community and the other half from the undergraduate student body of the University of Peradeniya, an arm of the national university system. Participants were asked to specify the number of same-sex and opposite-sex friends with whom they discussed personal matters. One-way ANOVA first was used to consider gender differences in mean number of friends for the overall sample, and then again for community versus university students. In the overall sample, females reported a significantly smaller number of friends (8.5) than did males (12.3) (one-way ANOVA, $p > .001$; Silva, Lewis, & Sivayoganathan, 1996). When the total sample was disaggregated by gender and community, however, the results were as shown in Table 9.3.

TABLE 9.3 Mean Number of Friends in Sri Lanka

	DWM	DWF	UPM	UPF
Mean number of total friends	11.5	8.3**	13.0	8.7**
Mean number of same-sex friends	7.9	6.2	9.7	6.3**
Mean number of opposite-sex friends	3.5	1.7*	3.3	2.4

NOTES: Sample code: DWM = Deyannewela community male; DWF = Deyannewela community female; UPM = University of Peradeniya male; UPF = University of Peradeniya female.
*Difference significant at .05 level (one-way ANOVA);
**Differences significant at .001 level (one-way ANOVA).

➤●➤●➤

Pearson's r *correlation coefficient.* Pearson's *r* correlation coefficient, sometimes called Pearson's product moment correlation or simply Pearson's *r*, is a statistic used on data drawn from samples that indicates the degree of linear relationship between two variables measured on an interval or ratio scale. Pearson's *r* is expressed in values between +1.0 and −1.0. A Pearson's *r* of +1.0 indicates a perfect direct linear relationship between two variables, that is, one variable predicts the other directly. For example, a Pearson's *r* correlation coefficient of +.73 between educational status and household income indicates a direct relationship between educational status (high) and household income (high), or between educational status (low) and household income (low). A Pearson's *r* value of −1.0 predicts a perfect *inverse* linear relationship; for example, a Pearson's *r* of −.73 for the variables "occupational status" and "presence of health problems" indicates an inverse relationship between occupational status (low) and presence of health problems (high)—or vice versa.

MULTIVARIATE STATISTICS

Multivariate analytic techniques are used to establish relationships among multiple independent or predictor variables and independent variables. The most frequently used general procedure for multivariate analysis is multiple linear regression. Multiple linear regression allows researchers to examine the relationship of a set of continuous independent or predictor variables (e.g., age, years of education, and socioeconomic status) with a dependent continuous variable such as school performance (e.g., grades or attendance) or drug use (e.g., frequency of use of cigarettes or alcohol). Preferable conditions for multivariate analysis are a random (or at least systematic) sample; a normal distribution of the variable; continuous independent and dependent variables; and approximately equal variance of the dependent variable across all levels of the independent variable.

Sometimes, it is difficult for novice researchers to figure out how to write up results expressed in statistics. Following are some helpful hints. For continuous variables or measures (ordinal, interval, and ratio), we commonly say that "we use general linear models (GLM)" and that the standard procedure is "multiple regression of independent variables onto the continuous dependent measure." With reference to a specific study, we would say, "We will regress age, years of education, and socioeconomic status of the household (the independent variables) onto grades (dependent variable)." Our interest in using these procedures is in finding out which independent variables account for the most variance in the dependent variable.

The most desirable and commonly used procedure is hierarchical multiple regression (Cohen & Cohen, 1983) because it calls for entering independent variables into the equation sequentially in order of their hypothesized chronological order or perceived importance in predicting variance in the dependent variable. In the example above, if the researcher believed that socioeconomic status was the most important predictor of grades, that variable would be entered into the regression equation first, followed by the other two in order of importance. In this way, the researcher controls the analysis. If an entry step is both statistically significant and accounts for a reasonable amount of the variance (i.e., 1% or more), we say that the variable will be considered for inclusion in the statistical model that we are trying to build. Ironically, not all statistically significant findings necessarily account for as much as 1% of the variance in many studies. Hence, we recommend that both criteria be used.

There are other forms of regression analysis, such as that used in the analysis of the data collected from young women in Mauritius, where groupings of variables defined by major independent variable domains were entered into the regression equation as blocks.

EXAMPLE 9.8

ENTERING VARIABLES INTO A MULTIPLE REGRESSION EQUATION:
AN EXAMPLE FROM MAURITIUS[2]

 Definition: Stepwise regression is an exploratory analytic procedure used to identify sets of variables within preidentified cultural or conceptual domains that predict variance within the dependent variable

The formative ethnographic theory guiding a study of young women, work, and AIDS risk in Mauritius stated that a combination of factors associated with the Peer, Family, and Work independent variable domains would be important in predicting outcomes. Outcome or dependent variable domains were Sex Behavior, Values Regarding Premarital Sex, AIDS Knowledge and Condom Knowledge. Variables from each independent domain were identified using stepwise regression analyses. **Stepwise regression analysis** allowed researchers to specify independent variables that might be important in determining the scores of the dependent variables. SPSS was used to identify those independent variables that correlated best or accounted for the greatest amount of variance in each of the dependent variable domains listed above. The program then entered all other identified independent variables. The results were different in relation to each of the dependent variables. Below, we explain how we arrived at the results.

First, each of the major independent domains was disaggregated into blocks of variables that made conceptual sense. The end result was a refinement of the qualitative coding tree described in Chapters 4 and 10 (Figures 4.4b and 10.8). These blocks are organized below first by independent variable domains and then by dependent variable domains. Each of the variables named in the far column to the right was created and defined. Variables for which there was no variation were eliminated. The final list of blocked variables is displayed in Table 9.4. The coding tree for the qualitative text data in this study includes most of the same variables so that patterns of association could be explored in the text data while they were also being investigated in the quantitative data. Independent variable domains, factors, variables, and variable names are displayed in Table 9.4. Domains consisting of dependent variables, factors, variables, and variable names are shown in Table 9.5.

TABLE 9.4 Blocks of Independent Variables in the Mauritius Work, Sex Risk, and AIDS Study

Domain	Factor	Variable	Variable Name
Family	Family structure	Father's role in family	(FAROLE)[a]
		Mother's role in family	(MAROLE)
		Sibling structure	(SIBROLE)
	Family environment	Family approval of work	(FMAPPR)
		Family traditionality	(FTRAD)
		Family violence/restrictiveness	(FVIOL)
		Family problems	(FPROB)
		Hours of housework/work	(FCHOR)
		% of month's salary given to family	(FCONT)
		# of activities with family	(FAMACT)
		Working to support family	(FAMSUP)
Work	Characteristics	Work seniority	(WSEN)
		Education of respondent	(RED)
		Salary of respondent	(RSAL)
		Age at time of entry into workforce	(EPZAGE)
	Work environment	Knowing men at work	(KNOWMEN)
		Satisfaction with income	(SATINC)
		Trust of female workers	(FEMTRST)
Peers	Peer structure	Size of female peer net	(FEMNET)
		Activities with female friends	(FEMACT)
		Number of male friends	(MALENET)
		Activities with male friends	(MALEACT)
		Boyfriend	(BOY)
		Fiancé	(FIANCÉ)
		BF/GF/Fiancé activities	(FBACT)
	Peer environment	BF/Fiancé restrictiveness/violence	(FBVIOL)
		BF/Fiancé communication	(FBCOMM)

a. As an example of the way in which each variable was defined, FAROLE and MAROLE were ordinal scales constructed after the survey data were collected, each with three levels: mother/father absent, mother/father present but unwell, and mother/father present and well. SIBROLE was composed of four variables integrated into a single variable using factor analysis, which included number of children in the family, birth order of respondent, size of family, and whether or not one or more siblings worked in the industrial sector.

TABLE 9.5 Dependent Variable Domains With Associated Factors, Variables, and
Variable Names

Domain	Factor	Variable	Variable Name
Risk Behavior	Sex	Count of sex behaviors	(SEXCT)
Sex Values	Premarital sex values	Values about premarital sex	(VPMSEX)
AIDS	Knowledge	Level of AIDS knowledge	(AIDKNOW)
Condoms	Condom knowledge	Knowledge of condoms	(CONDKNOW)

Table 9.6 shows the relationships among independent domains, factors, and variables, and four dependent variables and factors after conducting preliminary stepwise regression analyses with all of the above variables. NS means "not statistically significant." SEXCT refers to number of sex behaviors; VPMSEX refers to values about premarital sex, AIDSKNOW refers to AIDS knowledge, and CONDKNOW refers to condom knowledge, as indicated in the table of variables and variable names. Table 9.6 indicates which of the main variables on the list, and which other variables drawn from the 72-question survey instrument, are correlated with the four dependent variables. All of the column variables listed were significantly correlated with the dependent variables in their column.

🌞 **Definition: Forced stepwise regression is used to test hypotheses regarding which variables predict the greatest amount of variance; researchers enter variables into the regression equation in order of their hypothesized or assumed importance based on researcher experience and prior data analysis (Cohen & Cohen, 1983)**

The next step in the analysis involved entering into a **forced stepwise regression** those variables hypothesized to be important, or demonstrated to be important, by the strength of the correlation or by the amount of variance they predicted in each of the dependent variables. For sexual activity (SEXCT), six variables were entered, starting with the one predicting the greatest amount of variance. Five were from the Peer domain, and one was from the Work domain. No variables were entered from the Family domain. For attitudes toward sex, six variables were entered: two from the Family domain and four from the Peer domain. For AIDS knowledge, five variables were entered: three from the Work domain and two from the Family domain. Finally, for condom knowledge, three variables were entered: one each from the Work, Peer, and Family domains.

The results were as follows: Only variables from the Peer domain predicted sexual activity. Important Peer variables were size of male and female network (FEMNET), activities

TABLE 9.6 Relationships Among Independent Domains and Dependent Variables

Predictor Set	SEXCT	VPMSEX	AIDKNOW	CONDKNOW
Family				
Family structure	NS	NS	FAROLE	NS
Family work	FCONT FMAPPR	FMAPPR	FAMSUP	FAMSUP
Family environment	Q32G[a] FTRAD FACT	FTRAD FBVIOL	FAMACT	FAMACT
Work				
Work structure	Q13[b] WSEN	NS	RAGE[c] EPZAGE	RAGE
Work environment	KNOWMEN Q18f[d]	NS	KNOWMEN	NS
Peer				
Female friend network	FEMACT FEMNET	FEMNET	FEMACT	FEMACT FEMPRI
Male friend network	MALEACT	MALENET	MALEACT	MALEACT
BF/fiancé network	FIANCE1	FIANCE1	FIANCE1	FIANCE1
BF/Fiancé Environment	FBOMM1 FBVIOL1	FBVIOL1	FBCOMM1	NS

a. Q32g is an item in Question 32 of the questionnaire. The question asks about characteristics of family interaction. Item g of the question asks the respondent to identify where on a 5-point Likert scale her family is, from 1 = *without problems* to 5 = *with problems*.

b. Q13 is a question that asks for the respondent's salary for the previous week.

c. RAGE refers to respondent's current age.

d. Q18f refers to Item f in a series of questions related to work satisfaction. The item asks respondents to state where they would place themselves on a 5-point Likert scale, with 1 = *strongly agree* and 5 = *strongly disagree,* in response to the statement "I am satisfied with the income I am earning."

with peers (FBACT), learning more about male peers at work (KNOWMEN), better communication with boyfriend or fiancé (FBCOMM), and more restrictive behavior from boyfriend or fiancé (FBVIOL).

Variables from the Family and Peer domain predicted values about premarital sex. In the Peer domain, larger male network (MALENET), greater range of activities with boyfriend or fiancé (FBACT), and better communication with a boyfriend or fiancé (FBCOMM) predicted a more positive attitude toward premarital sex. In the Family domain, the less traditional the family (FTRAD), and the more the family disapproved of work in the EPZ (FMAPPR), the more positive the attitude toward premarital sex.

Variance in AIDS knowledge was predicted by variables in the Family and Work domains but not in the Peer domain. In the Work domain, higher education (RAGE), knowing more men through work, and older age at entry into the industrial work-force (EPZAGE) predicted more AIDS knowledge. In the Family domain, the presence and health of the father (FAROLE) and more activities with the family (FAMACT) predict more AIDS knowledge.

Little of the variance in condom knowledge was predicted by any of the variables. Only one variable from each of the domains was entered into the regression equation—RAGE (Work), FBACT (Peer), and FAMACT (Family). This completed the hierarchical and stepwise regression analyses. These results, coupled with the examination of blocks of text coded with the same variable names, provided the basis for interpretation, which we will discuss in the next chapter (Schensul et al., 1994, pp. 86-128).

The case study above describes how a statistical model was constructed from ethnographically informed survey data based on

- An initial formative ethnographic theoretical model
- The elaboration of the model into factors and variables based on exploratory and semistructured data collection
- The transformation of the revised model into an ethnographic survey
- The return to the model for analysis of survey data

Logistic Regression

The last form of multiple regression analysis to be mentioned here is logistic regression. Logistic regression is used when dependent variables are dichotomous or when they have been transformed from a continuum to a dichotomy because the curve is not normal, that is, the curve is skewed because variables are not distributed normally (symmetrically) in the population. Logistic regression requires that independent variables also be converted to categorical variables subsequent to entry into regression equations. Logistic regression is viewed as increasingly useful by researchers who have come to believe that most variables in which we are interested in social science research are ranked (ordinal) rather than absolute (interval or ratio). A description of logistic regression and instructions regarding how to use this analytic technique are beyond the scope of this book. For assistance in deciding whether to convert dependent variables into categorical variables and how to conduct logistic regression, readers are advised to refer to other texts (cf. Babbie, 1995).

Table 9.7 displays a summary of the statistical procedures we have described in this chapter. Now, in the final section, we discuss suggestions for integrating qualitative (text and observation) data; survey data; and data collected via other means, such as network research, social-spatial mapping, and elicitation techniques described in Books 3 and 4.

TRIANGULATING QUALITATIVE, SURVEY, AND OTHER FORMS OF QUANTITATIVE DATA

By this time, readers will probably recognize that ethnographic survey data are not likely to be collected unless considerable exploratory work has been done. There are four main ways in which other forms of data can be integrated with ethnographic survey data.

Using qualitative data to inform the development of theoretical models. We have discussed in detail both in this book and in Book 2 some ways of using ethnographic text data from observations and semistructured interviews to inform the development of the theoretical model guiding the survey. We refer readers to Book 2 for more information on this topic.

Cross Reference: See Book 2, Chapters 5-8, for the collection of qualitative and survey data to inform theoretical modeling

TABLE 9.7 Statistical Techniques and Their Uses

Procedure: Descriptive Statistics	Purpose	Description	Uses
Frequency distribution (includes the definition and description of subgroups within the population)	Portrays modal pattern and range of variation	Raw scores ranked from low to high; grouped scores; frequency of appearance of scores	Decide on types of variable transformations; describe profiles and variation in the population
Central tendency: mean	Defines average of a set of scores	Add scores and divide by number of scores	Describes the predominant trend at the interval or ratio level
Central tendency: median	Defines the midpoint in a range of scores	Rank scores; find the midpoint. Divides a distribution of scores exactly in half	Describes the predominant trend at the ordinal, interval, and ratio levels
Central tendency: mode	Defines the most frequent score	Scores or group scores are ranked and frequencies established; the modal score or group score has the highest frequency	Describes the predominant trend at the nominal, ordinal, interval, and ratio levels
Range	Difference between highest and lowest scores for a variable	Highest and lowest scores	Describes the spread of scores to show the extent of variability in the population
Variance	Calculates the average of the summed squared deviation of each score from the mean	Standard deviation squared	Used instead of standard deviation in inferential statistical analysis
Standard deviation	A measure of the spread of scores around a mean		Summarizes variability in a population; used for descriptive purposes instead of the range
t-test	Compares means for two unrelated samples (interval and ratio)	Compares means	Used to determine whether there are statistically significant differences in the means of two independent or two related populations
Paired t-test	Compares means for two related samples (pre- and posttests)		

Chi-square	Determines whether the *relationship between two nominal variables* is greater than chance	Bivariate (2×2) table with independent or predictor variable at the top and dependent variable or variable whose variance is to be predicted, along the side	Explanation of the relationship between these variables such that one is logically seen as "causing" or "predicting" the second; tests covariation between two nominal variables
Fisher's exact test	Determines whether the *relationship between two nominal variables* is greater than chance	Identical to chi-square	For use with 2×2 tables where frequencies for any cell in the table are less than 5; used most often with small samples; does not suggest direction of relationship
Gamma	Measures the association between two *ordinal variables*	3×3 table; formula is same ranked pairs – opposite ranked pairs/same ranked pairs + opposite ranked pairs	Tells whether knowing the ranking of pair of people on one variable enhances capacity to predict ranking on a second variable
Pearson's product moment correlation (r)	Determines whether there is a statistically significant relationship between two *interval or ratio* measures	Based on guessing the value of one variable by knowing the other	Can be used with interval/interval variables, interval and ordinal variables, interval and nominal variables
Eta (η)	Considers the relationship between groupings of means within a population and a continuous dependent variable	Groups means based on researcher opinion; establishes means of subgroups; relates means to outcome or dependent variable; arrives at a total probability score	Used to test covariation between nominal and interval variables and between ordinal and interval variables; is the only statistic that addresses nonlinear relationships with interval variables
ANOVA	Tests the hypothesis that the *means of* two or more populations on a single variable are not equal to one another	Compares means of two or more independent populations on a single variable	Inferential: Used to compare group means in two or more groups within the same population or between two different populations at two points in time (e.g., random samples of a target population at Times 1, 2, and 3)
Factor analysis	Assesses associations among continuous variables to determine statistically defined variable groupings (factors)		A means of "data reduction"; can reduce many variables to scales consisting of similar continuous variables; factors are usually not predetermined but allowed to emerge from the data

TABLE 9.7 Continued

Procedure: Descriptive Statistics	Purpose	Description	Uses
One-way ANOVA	Explores the effect of *one* categorical independent variable on a continuous dependent variable	Requires a predictive model with at least one categorical independent variable and one continuous dependent variable	Inferential: Used to determine relationships between categorical and continuous variables
Two-way ANOVA	Tests the effect of *two* categorical independent variables on a continuous dependent variable	Requires a predictive model with at least two categorical independent variables and one continuous dependent variable	Inferential: Used to calculate relationships between categorical and continuous variables
Multiple-way ANOVA	Tests the effects of *more than two* categorical independent variables on a continuous dependent variable	Requires a predictive model with more than two categorical independent variables and one continuous dependent variable	Permits an examination of the effects of multiple independent categorical variables on a continuous dependent variable
Regression analysis	Association between two interval or ratio variables: y is a function of x	y "causes" x so the value of y determines the value of x	Regression analysis establishes the regression equation representing the geometric line that comes closest to the distribution of points on the x-y axis—with values of x, we can predict values of y
Multiple regression analysis (simple, stepwise, and hierarchical linear modeling)	Association between multiple interval or ratio independent (antecedent) variables and a dependent variable	Multiple independent variables account for more of the variance than does a single independent variable	When a dependent variable is affected simultaneously by several independent variables
Path analysis	Assumes that the values of one variable are *caused* by the values of another	Must identify independent and dependent variables (cause and effect)	Considers patterns of relationships among variables and calculates the strength of the relationships in a multivariate model

Using qualitative text data to explore quantitative associations or correlations qualitatively. This step requires that the coding system for text data be developed in advance of the ethnographic survey, and that at least the major coding categories (domains, factors, subfactors, and even variables) be used for both purposes. To maximize the linkage between qualitative and quantitative relationships, researchers would then search coded text for blocks of text that display multiple codes consistent with the correlations being pursued quantitatively.

Using the study above, researchers could search the coded text databases for the intersection of text blocks coded as FAMILY and SEXCT to find descriptions of the relationship in the text data. Or, with a more refined coding system, they could search for the interaction of family activities (FAMACT)—a variable—and SEXCT. Programs such as AFTER, ETHNOGRAPH, or NUD·IST allow up to 12 or more codes to be applied to a single block of text. Thus, at least theoretically, depending on the detail with which coding categories are applied, it is possible to find text blocks that reflect qualitatively or descriptively the most complex quantitative equations.

Using text data to develop new conceptual guidelines. By exploring ethnographic text data using methods outlined in earlier chapters of this book, we can develop new conceptual models that can guide data analysis in new and unpredicted ways. This approach is useful even when the formative theoretical model is well developed, because, when read thoroughly, high-quality text data often reveal new insights. They have the potential for generating interesting ideas and questions that can be tested with matched survey data in ways never anticipated in the original study.

Using quantitative results to guide additional qualitative investigation. Unexpected correlations and associations found in the survey data can raise important issues that can be addressed and understood better by returning to the ethnographic text data for interpretation (Schensul, Munoz-Laboy, & Bojko, 1998; Schensul et al., 1994). In a study of health needs and health care utilization in the Puerto Rican community of Hartford, ethnographer Stephen Schensul and activist Maria Borrero made the unanticipated discovery that high numbers of Puerto Rican women of childbearing age were turning to sterilization as a form of birth control. This led to further analysis of in-depth interview and narrative data, focus groups with women, and a review of the history of fertility control among Puerto Ricans in Puerto Rico to discover the reasons for this unexpected pattern (Gonzales, Barrera, Guarnaccia, & Schensul, 1982).

Other forms of data can be used in conjunction with ethnographic survey data in the same ways. Quantitative data collected on a single person's personal networks can be entered into data files as information about his or her network characteristics. These vary with the study but generally include targeted behavioral exchanges as well as network variables such as size, percentage of kin members, average age, and so on. Ethnographic descriptions of observed networks in action can help to quantify network questions, confirm network data obtained through questionnaires, or describe the context within which ego-centered networks function. Similarly, networks discovered through in-depth interviews and observations can help to explain the history and functioning of components of full relational networks identified quantitatively through survey research.

Elicitation techniques described in Books 2 and 3 are designed to capture information on the way people organize and think about cultural domains. Data obtained through listings, for example, offer an important opportunity for identifying cultural items or units within subdomains; they also provide the framework for detailed discus-

Cross Reference:
See Book 4, Chapter 1, on network research

Cross Reference:
See especially Borgatti's chapter on elicitation techniques in Book 3

sions about cultural domains that enrich both further analysis and other dimensions of the study. Finally, as with frequencies and measures of central tendency, multidimensional scaling and cluster analysis performed on sorted items seek cultural consensus and, at the same time, reveal intragroup variation, which is important to explore further both qualitatively and through survey research.

Cultural consensus data can confirm other study results. We had reason to believe, for example, that AIDS was not a salient subject among teens in Hartford. By using listing exercises, we confirmed that AIDS was not mentioned in most of the groups that were asked to identify major areas of concern to urban teens. Items drawn from the listing exercise, sorted, and subjected to multidimensional scaling and cluster analysis revealed that AIDS was located in a cluster of its own, apart from other issues, including those related to sexuality and sexual health (Schensul, 1998-1999).

The activities and behaviors of social network members, patterns of accessing health care and other community resources, and school choices at a time of diversification and privatization are examples of issues often addressed through survey data. The location of individuals in relation to social activities and institutions is critical to understanding how and why they use resources. GIS and other forms of mapping, described by Ellen Cromley in Book 4, are tools that help researchers to array their data in space, revealing patterns otherwise not noticeable.

Cross Reference: See Book 4, Chapter 2, on spatial mapping

Resolving Differences Between Quantitative and Qualitative Results

Different approaches to the collection of data may produce different as well as complementary results. Information obtained from in-depth interviews and observations may expand what we can learn from surveying, but they often tell a slightly different story. For example, research results from a random sample of 500 young women surveyed in the Mauritius study produced somewhat lower rates of penetrative sex and higher counts of oral sex than did counts from the 90 women who were interviewed using a semistructured interview (Schensul, 1994; Schensul et al., 1994). This led researchers to conclude one of two possibilities: either women were more comfortable reporting oral sex on a survey than in person because it was a very intimate behavior, or there were slight differences between women in the two samples. Similarly, data collected in field observations about whether safety measures such as bleach were used to protect against HIV infection sometimes contradicted results obtained from surveys with the same people who had been observed in the field. Respondents were more likely to report safe behavior (i.e., to tell interviewers what they wanted to hear) even when they knew the interviewers had actually observed them engaging in risky drug use in the field. As we said earlier, putting together the results of ethnographic data collection is like completing a puzzle.

In the instances mentioned above, the pieces of the puzzle do not quite fit. We would not suggest that they must always fit. Instead, we urge ethnographers to continue their data collection and to try to explain the differences. Often, explanation will provide greater insight into cultural patterning.

Furthermore, to understand differences (and similarities) in results, researchers should also consider

- The purpose of the data collection method (explanation through collection of in-depth information vs. explanation through the collection of the most valid data possible with a large sample, via ethnographically informed surveys)
- The nature of the information being collected, for example, how personal or embarrassing it is for people to discuss it openly in the setting
- Who is collecting the information

- How well the researcher is able to collect the information
- How well the researcher is able to establish a relationship with respondents
- The degree of comfort established between researcher and respondent or participant in the study
- The limitations and advantages of one form of data collection over another

SUMMARY

We have now talked about cleaning, crunching, and analyzing both qualitative and quantitative ethnographic data. Remaining are the tasks of organizing data for presentation and determining what the presented data mean to a variety of audiences. In Chapter 10, we discuss presentation and preliminary interpretation of data; Chapter 11 is devoted to methods for organizing final interpretation of findings and determining the significance of the results to numerous constituencies interested in the research.

NOTES

1. The Scholastic Aptitude Test (SAT) is an examination given in the United States to assess aptitude for college entrance.

2. Readers may note that several of the variables in the regression analysis are ordinal (ranked) measures. Researchers differ as to whether ordinal measures can be used in regression analyses. In this case, statistician Bonnie Nastasi and researcher Steve Schensul, who performed the analyses, believed that these procedures were appropriately executed.

10 ━●━●━●━

FINE-TUNING RESULTS: ASSEMBLING COMPONENTS, STRUCTURES, AND CONSTITUENTS

GETTING STARTED

Structural or constitutive analysis involves linking together or finding consistent relationships among patterns, components, constituents, and structures. As the outlines and contents of structures and constituents become more and more distinct, they become part of a clear portrait of the phenomenon under study. However, ethnographers often find it difficult to figure out how to assemble these parts into a full story. They have developed a number of strategies for getting started, ranging from the rather mundane and routine to the artistic. Perhaps the most im- portant point to remember at this stage of the process is that researchers can assemble constituents deductively—from the top down—or inductively—from the bottom up—or some combination of moving back and forth between induction and deduction. In this chapter, we review a number of strategies for initiating the construction of analytically informed stories and beginning the organization of results into a full-fledged ethnographic portrait.

Definition:
Structural or constituent analysis involves integrating all of the various components or constituent parts of the study

LOOK AT THE THEORETICAL FRAMEWORK

🐰 **Cross Reference:** See Book 2, Chapters 2 and 3; also Chapter 4 of this volume

If researchers had a relatively well-developed formative ethnographic theory at the outset of the study, the process of assembling and integrating components would, to some degree, be structured deductively in advance. A study that used such a deductive approach based on a formative theoretical framework, then shifted to bottom-up induction, was Schensul's study in Mauritius.

EXAMPLE 10.1 ━●◆━●◆━

WRITING UP RESEARCH BY BEGINNING WITH A FORMATIVE
THEORETICAL MODEL: SEX RISK IN MAURITIUS

The formative theoretical model for research on young women, work, and risk in Mauritius (Figure 4.4a) identified three domains—family, peers, and work—that researchers believed would be important in shaping sexual beliefs, attitudes, and behaviors. Exploratory ethnography resulted in an elaboration of these domains into a coding tree or taxomony (Figures 10.7 and 10.8), which was developed further through semistructured interviews with a sample of 90 unmarried young women and 30 unmarried young men. The results of these two data sources contributed to a further elaboration of the coding tree and the identification of items and variables that were included in a structured interview schedule. The process of assembling components and writing up the data followed the guide established by coding trees. For example, one section of the monograph summarized both qualitative and quantitative data related to family. Paragraphs or larger sections of the write-up focused on different items and factors in the taxonomy, and the section as a whole covered a description and analysis of all of the items included in the coding tree for that domain—family structure, family health, family work history, family activities, family socialization practices, and so on—with greater emphasis on those that seemed to be related more specifically to sexuality. The quantitative analysis identified statistically significant associations among variables, and the qualitative data illustrated those examples and helped to explain why the associations existed. This process was both inductive and deductive.

━●◆━●◆━

In contrast, some exploratory or descriptive research begins with questions. Researchers first identify a problem, question, or topic as the central domain. At least initially, some of the variables or conditions associated with the central domain or problem may be identified or predicted in advance of the study, but many more may emerge in the course of data collection. Furthermore, it is likely that many additional new domains associated with the original set will be identified and explored as the study progresses. The purpose of the study, then, becomes to identify new domains associated with the topic or problem, describe them, find associations among them, and interpret the relationships. One such study is described in Example 10.2; it began with questions rather than with a formative theoretical framework.

EXAMPLE 10.2

UNDERSTANDING CHILDREN'S ACTIVITY LEVELS: WRITING UP EXPLORATORY RESEARCH

Researchers Schensul, Diaz, and Woolley were interested in finding out in which activities Latino children children aged 7 to 10 were involved and what might account for the patterns that were expected to emerge. To find out, they conducted listing exercises with classrooms of children in the target age group. They asked children to brainstorm all of the activities in which they were involved. Researchers probed for the times when and the locations where these activities occurred, asking such questions as "What about weekends?" or "What about at home, or in the backyard, or on the back steps?" This exercise produced a listing of 62 items that ranged from helping with housework to athletic exercises after school. These activities then were reconstituted into an "activities recall" instrument in which nearly 80 young students and their primary caregivers participated; they also took part in a semistructured interview.

The recall activity provided information on the central concept: children's activity outputs. The interview schedule provided additional data on a variety of factors associated with differential involvement in activities and perceived differential output. The results were descriptive, although researchers also generated some predictive hypotheses, including the idea that mothers' activity patterns established norms for daughters but not for sons.

REVIEW THE RESEARCH QUESTIONS

One of the most important—but often forgotten—ways to begin the write-up of ethnographic data is to go back to the research question and focus on the most important questions that the study is intended to answer. This provides critical clues and directions as to which parts of the study can be written up first. This is the approach LeCompte took to the Learning Circle study.

EXAMPLE 10.3

WRITING UP RESULTS FROM THE RESEARCH QUESTIONS: THE LEARNING CIRCLE STUDY

Initially, LeCompte was stymied when faced with mountains of data from the Learning Circle study. Then, she remembered that the original questions to be addressed in the evaluation portion of the study had to do with the impact of the program on student achievement and self-esteem. She began by assembling all of the results they had amassed for student performance, including teacher grades, standardized tests, classroom teacher-made tests, and the developmental records maintained by the Learning Circle teachers, and she wrote a section of the report addressing those matters.

Subsequently, after describing the results of the study with respect to the outcomes (which we referred to earlier as the *dependent variable domain*), LeCompte had many choices. She could review the remainder of the data to identify and describe the causes—anticipated or unanticipated—of the outcomes as defined above. Or, she could consider to which other aspects of the setting student achievement and self-esteem might relate and describe these. Or, she could examine the data to determine whether there were differences in perception of parents, teachers, and students with regard to outcomes, thereby offering alternatives to the standard outcome measures itemized above.

CREATE VIGNETTES

A look at the initial research questions also can give hints as to how an initial portrayal could be formulated. For example, if the study involves determining typical behavior, such as "a day in the life" or "a typical case," ethnographers can begin by organizing their data into **vignettes**. Vignettes often are snapshots or short descriptions of events or people that evoke the overall picture that the ethnographer is trying to paint. This is why Van Maanen (1988) calls them "impressionist tales"; they are stories that can be told quickly and that mark and make memorable the fieldwork experience because they reconstruct in dramatic form people or events the ethnographer regards as especially notable and, hence, reportable.

There are three kinds of vignettes: normative depictions, or what Van Maanen calls "realist tales"; dramas, or what Van Maanen calls "impressionistic accounts"; and critical events/stories, or "confessional tales."

Definition:
A vignette is a short dramatic description, some of which typify, creating a composite of all of the people or events studied; others dramatize a person, act, event, or activity so as to catch the attention of the reader; and still others summarize a biography, event, or other phenomenon

---

Types of Vignettes

- Normative depictions
- Dramas
- Critical events

Normative depictions are attempts to present in a forceful and succinct way a description that the ethnographer considers to be an authentic cultural representation. They usually are written in the third person; many of them describe "a typical day in the life of the people I am studying," "a typical person of the type I am studying," or "a typical performance of the activity in which I am interested." Elias Martinez's description in Example 10.4 is an excerpt from such a normative vignette that describes the daily activities of Latino immigrant schoolchildren in a mountain community.

EXAMPLE 10.4 ➤•➤•➤

A NORMATIVE DEPICTION: THE DAY BEGINS AT SNOW MOUNTAIN ELEMENTARY SCHOOL

Mornings dawn crisply in the high mountain valleys. The whole valley seems ener-
gized with the expectation of a new day of work for many of the inhabitants of a
trailer city, La Sierra Trailer Court, located about two miles from the edge of town.
Soon, the school buses would be arriving and the children would begin another day
of school. The trailer park is abuzz with sounds of cars warming up or others having
the ice scraped from their windshields. Parents, older siblings, or relatives make sure
that the children are up in the darkness of winter mornings and are prepared for
another day of school. Mornings at the bus stop are quiet. The children, still sleepy
from the night before, begin to arrive from their respective trailers. The trailer park
is large, and some have walked nearly a quarter of a mile from their trailer. As the bus
arrives, hurried goodbyes are exchanged, and the children's mood seems to change;
their energy level increases, and they begin to chat with each other in anticipation of
another day at school. This morning, as on most mornings, the parking lot of the
school is teeming with activity. Automobiles, minivans, and sport utility vehicles line
up to discharge children as directed by a teacher or the principal. Up on the hillside,
away from the bustle, five buses unload the immigrant children from across the valley.
Teachers meet them and escort them to a staging area on the playground so they can
await their march into the school building. With backpacks flying, children hurry to
their assigned places. Latino children stop to greet whomever happens to be around
who can speak Spanish. They seem anxious to maintain continuity with someone
who can speak their language. . . . The more ebullient Latino students call out to any
Latino person and engage in banter. Conversations in Spanish can be heard as the
Latino children call out to give each other encouragement for the day ahead. Then
begins the separation.

The energy that was created in the short busride down the mountain is soon
diffused as the children are separated into groups lined up behind their respective
teachers. Some are lucky enough to have two or three other Latino children in their
class with whom they can talk in Spanish. Others are not so lucky. They join classes
where they might be the only Spanish speaker. These students adopt a subdued
demeanor or continue to talk with another Latino student in the lines near them, but
not for long. As soon as the children have gathered, the teacher marches them to the
classrooms to begin another day of learning. (Martinez, 1998, pp. 237-240)

➤•➤•➤

Martinez's description continues, following the children through the day. He traces how they are separated first from each other and then from regular classroom instruction when they are sent to several kinds of special language instruction—instruction that is related only infrequently to what the non-immigrant students are being taught. He argues that this process destroys educational continuity and prevents Latino children from developing both social competence and academic skills in English.

Because ethnographers look for patterns and structures, **Key point** *overall themes and shared meanings, normative depictions —as composites of what people say, do, believe, or are characterized by—can come close to an accurate and full picture of a cultural scene.* By contrast, dramas are vignettes that say to the reader, "OK, now that I've gotten your attention with this exciting story, let me back away from it and tell you about what happened every day in more normal circumstances." Below is such a drama; it describes the violation of an important norm whose existence became very clear because of the violation.

EXAMPLE 10.5   ➤●➤●➤

IDENTIFYING AN UNBREACHABLE RULE IN PUBLIC SCHOOLS: TAKING ATTENDANCE

During a faculty meeting in December, the new high school math teacher suddenly blurted out, "So, what do you do with all these little blue slips for student absences? I thought it was too much trouble to hand them in each period, so I've just sort of been taking attendance at the beginning of the day and ignoring the ones for the rest of the day." A shocked silence filled the room, broken after a few long minutes by the Spanish teacher, who said, "You know, these are really important. A child could show up at the beginning of the day. But if they decide to leave at 10 o'clock to go to the restaurant across that busy street outside for a snack, and get hit by a car and hurt or even kidnapped, we wouldn't know where that child is. And we are responsible. Legally responsible! In fact, the last teacher who saw that child is responsible. If that last teacher were you, it's *your* neck! That's why we take attendance after *every* class. And I suggest you do the same."

Critical event vignettes also catch the reader's attention, but they depict scenes that were turning points in the researcher's understanding or that changed the direction of events in the field site.

EXAMPLE 10.6   ━━●━◆━●━◆━

A CRITICAL EVENT: THE FACULTY CHANGES ITS STANCE ON ARTS FOCUS

Even after a year and a half, the Arts Focus program at Centerline Middle School was perceived by the non-arts teachers to be something of an intruder. It was received warmly by some and with distrust by others, but it was embraced by no one but administrators and the four participating teachers. A constant source of low morale among the arts teachers was the lack of support, the disinterest, and the sometimes open hostility they experienced from other teachers. The message seemed to be that art was nice, but it was a frill and certainly not the responsibility of non-arts teachers.

During the first year, the four arts teachers did all of the recruiting of students, all of the media publicity, and all of the visits to parents and other schools in the district, trying to stimulate interest. The faculty's disinterested stance changed dramatically, however, at a faculty meeting in December, just before the enrollment period was to begin. The old principal had not been very enthusiastic about the arts program. In contrast, the new Centerline principal had been a band director and was convinced that the best thing the school had was its Arts Focus program—and that without it, the school would be in danger of closure because of dropping enrollment. So, he proposed that the other teachers help out with recruiting, perhaps by talking about how strong the academic program at Centerline was at the Spring Parents' Meeting. These meetings were an annual community event at which parents chose which public school their child would attend. Each school put on a good "show," trying to make their program appear irresistible and appealing to parents.

Not a single academic area teacher at Centerline volunteered to help. One person grumbled that art was not his responsibility. At that point, the assistant principal stood and began to write on the blackboard. Reminding the faculty that the arts program had been initiated to encourage new enrollment, and that 3 years ago, enrollment at Centerline had dropped so precipitously that school district officials were about to close the school, she quickly sketched out the current and projected enroll-

ment figures, with and without the Arts Focus students. Her figures made it clear that the additional 165 Arts Focus students helped—but that the school still was under-enrolled for the size of the faculty—given that teachers were assigned to schools based on enrollment size. Furthermore, the school had a capacity of 630 students, and current enrollment was 420. As the school board tried to cut costs, underenrolled schools were being closed, and surplus teachers were in danger of losing their jobs. "This means," said the assistant principal, "that each of you will have to bring in at least one new student next year if we aren't going to lose faculty." Silence fell.

Then, a sixth-grade teacher said, "You know, our sixth grade is so small this year that all of the sixth-grade teachers now are teaching part-time. Next year, the seventh grade will be small, and the seventh-grade teachers will be part-time, too. And the next year, it'll be eighth grade. The Arts Focus teachers kept our school open for us last year, and we never even noticed. This year, we've got to go out and help them or we won't have *any* jobs in 3 years!" Another silence fell.

Suddenly, three teachers volunteered the entire team of sixth-grade teachers to make presentations at Parents' Night. Others volunteered help with designing news-paper advertisements to publicize the program. The rest of the meeting was devoted to planning ways that the whole school could participate in recruiting Arts Focus students. And for the first time in 18 months, the Arts Focus teachers began to feel as though they were strongly supported as a crucial element in their school.

Dramas and critical-event vignettes should be used with caution because they generally portray extreme, unique, or unusual events rather than patterns, and they are not *typical.* Focusing on extraordinary or extreme events can create a biased picture of the daily life that the ethnographer usually attempts to portray, unless it is the existence of such an extreme case that makes the pattern emerge clearly. For example, sometimes, an ethnographer cannot really learn what the rules are in given situations unless somebody violates them. The dramatic event depicted in Example 10.5 above does not portray a typical event, but it does demonstrate what the rules are in the context of a major violation of norms.

Key point

Too many novice ethnographers think that their analysis and write-up are finished once they have summarized their data or told the story of each and every one of their informants. Unfortunately, by themselves, vignettes and summaries are not the end product of the ethnography. They merely serve as "advance cognitive organizers" that tell enough of the whole story so that the reader can follow subsequent and more complete narratives or arguments that demonstrate how the vignette constitutes evidence for the position the ethnographer is taking or the explanations presented previously.

WRITE SOME HISTORY

Another way to begin a write-up is to trace the history of whatever has been studied. Often, research results are not very easy to understand unless some of the events that preceded or gave rise to the phenomenon that the ethnographer is trying to describe are made clear. Writing down that history is a good way to put some text on paper and organize both one's own thoughts and the structure of the write-up itself. These can include the history of a program, a culture, or an institution. For example, Liane Brouillette began her report of current school reforms in a community in the western United States by describing the growth and change in the community from a frontier agricultural and mining area to the suburban fringe of a major metropolitan area. She used this background to trace the growth of the school district and the changes in educational practice wrought by the philosophies of the three school superintendents that the district had had since its founding. This historical material formed the background for understanding current conflicts between various community groups over the purposes of education, methods of instruction, ways to finance schools, and the administrative styles required for effective leadership in the district (Brouillette, 1996).

DESCRIBE A SOCIAL PROCESS

Ethnographers also can begin by describing social processes. LeCompte and Holloway began part of the report for Arts Focus by describing the recruitment and enrollment procedures used by Centerline Middle School to fill places in the arts program; in so doing, they found that this description also made considerable reference to bureaucratic snafus; areas of conflict and misunderstanding between the school district administration, the school principal, the teachers, and the students' parents; and factors that impeded accurate and effective communication about the program to the community at large. The researchers then wrote up each of these areas separately to become sections of the finished report.

CREATE SUMMARIES OF INTERVIEW
OR SURVEY RESULTS

We have already indicated that ethnographers sometimes begin their analysis by working with data that are easy to code. Similarly, they often begin the write-up by working with summaries of the same kinds of data—tests, interviews, questionnaires, and surveys—because computers can help the researcher produce summaries of the data rather quickly. These summaries can be described in narrative form, formatted graphically (see the section on creating a display), and presented as a significant section of the report.

CREATE COLLECTIONS OF QUOTATIONS

Just as ethnographers can write up summaries of quantifiable data—as just described—ethnographers also can use computers—or scissors, tape, and glue—to create collections of quotes from texts, documents, or interviews. Placed together, these materials often demonstrate patterns or structures that, when described in narrative form, can be useful first chunks of a report.

EXAMPLE 10.7 ━━●━━●━━

STARTING WITH SUMMARIES OF DOCUMENTS
OR SURVEY RESULTS: EXPLAINING EMPOWERMENT

During the early 1990s, LeCompte and Bennett de Marrais began to examine the wide use of the term *empowerment* by educational reformers. Both researchers had done work on the use of the term, and both realized that although teachers, administrators, policymakers, and public figures all sprinkled the term liberally throughout their speeches and policy statements, there was little consistency within or among these groups as to its meaning. LeCompte and Bennett de Marrais began their write-up of research with a listing of quotations from public figures—even military command- ers—and educators, each of which used the term *empowerment* in a different way. Then, they reported results from ethnographic interviews asking members of differ- ent populations in the school district that LeCompte was studying what they thought the term meant to them. Wide-ranging variation in these responses, as well as the public statements, set the stage for an article that presented the remainder of an ethnographic study examining the term's use and its current value as a "slogan system" (Apple, 1995) in public discourse (LeCompte & Bennett de Marrais, 1992).

CREATE A CONCEPTUAL FRAMEWORK AND DRAW A GRAPHIC PICTURE OF IT

Researchers also can create conceptual frameworks into whose categories they sort data as if the data were being placed into "bins" (Miles & Huberman, 1984) or boxes. Vadeboncoeur's three-category conceptual framework de- picted in Figure 4.1 is such a framework; in her report, she first provided the diagram in graphic form and then fol- lowed the diagram with a rather lengthy narrative descrip- tion that defined the origins of each category and what it represented, the kinds of data that she sorted into each category and why they were sorted that way, and then how

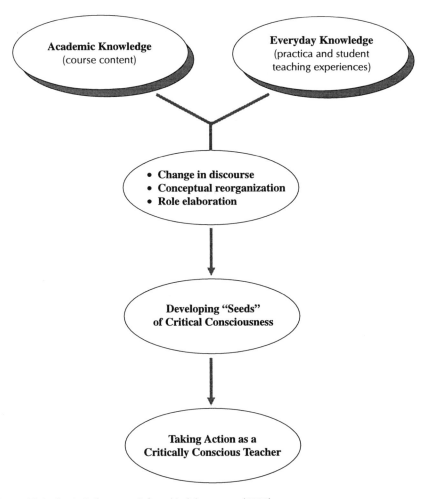

Figure 10.1. Analytic framework from Vadeboncoeur (1998).

the diagram was related to the reality of the program under study. Later, she created a more complex diagram (see Figure 10.1) to display her analytic strategies; this diagram, too, was written up as described above. The process is similar to that described in operationalization or "building formative theory" in Book 2, but occurs after the data are collected (i.e., inductively) rather than before.

USE STANDARD NARRATIVE FORM

Ethnographers also often decide in advance to use one of the basic narrative traditions or genres common in Western society (see Hayden White, cited in Clifford, 1990, p. 55). Sometimes, this involves telling a story by structuring it chronologically from the earliest events to the most recent, and including in it an abstract form of beginning (such as the "once upon a time" that begins many children's stories); an orientation to the time and place where the phenomenon occurred; presentation of the "cast of characters" or people involved; a description of complicating actions, or what actually happened (analogous to the plot in a story); a coda, or statement of what happened as a result of the complicating action or events; a resolution or solution to problems identified or encountered in the plot line; and some evaluation statements, which tell how the writer felt about what was happening, or compare the events to others that did or might have occurred (adapted from Mishler, 1986).

Another form of write-up involves so-called technical writing, which gets to the point quickly. Rather than extensive narrative description, technical writing relies on succinct summaries of data and requires the presentation of a summary of results first, followed by a body of evidence supporting the credibility, validity, reliability, and authenticity of those results.

BORROW A NARRATIVE FORM FROM THE PEOPLE WHOM YOU ARE STUDYING

The kinds of writing or presentation genres described above have been criticized because of their closeness to Western ways of thinking and communicating. Some researchers argue that presenting non-Western ideas in a Western format destroys their meaning (see Said, 1978; Spivak, 1988; Trinh, 1989). In an unusual study, Karen Von Gunten analyzed the stories told by North American Lakota Indians in a description of American Indian ways of thinking about knowledge and learning. These stories are told on various levels: They constitute entertainment, they are told to teach young Lakota about their religion and preferred practices, and they are also told as a means of social control. Evoking a particular story often reminds the hearers of cultural norms and practices that they should follow but do not; they also can serve to reinforce ideals and norms or present metaphysical interpretations of events. Von Gunten presented her data first in the metaphoric and narrative formats used by the Lakota people themselves because she felt that the standard narrative format of most Western writing—see Mishler's typology described in this book in Chapter 5—was absent from and inappropriate for the Lakota stories with which she worked. She then reorganized the format to one more comfortable to academics, school administrators, and educational policymakers—people more accustomed to concrete and chronological narratives—who then could use the study's findings to design educational materials more suitable to Lakota children than are the mainstream, European American-oriented ones currently in use (Von Gunten, 1999).

DEVELOP A METAPHOR

Ethnographers often begin their write-up by inventing a metaphor or image that captures the sense or evokes the meaning that the writer is trying to convey, using it to create a link between the known metaphor and the more unfamiliar phenomenon that the ethnographer is trying to describe.

EXAMPLE 10.8

WITCHCRAFT AS A METAPHOR FOR UNIVERSITY PROCEDURES

Frank Lutz (1982) used the metaphor of witchcraft to structure his study of university faculty, explaining procedures for obtaining tenure and getting promoted in terms of rituals and rites, and the documents used to substantiate claims for academic excellence to charms and fetishes.

━●━●━●━

 Key point *It is important to remember that the metaphor is not the phenomenon itself;* university faculty in the United States usually do not practice witchcraft! However, the practices of witchcraft are well enough understood—at least at some level—by nonuniversity people that understanding of the arcane and sometimes bewildering procedures undergone by professors can be assisted by comparing them humorously to the rituals and procedures used by shamans. A

Key point caution should be noted with regard to metaphors: *To make sense to the reader, the item that is being used metaphorically must be familiar and acceptable to the audience whom the ethnographer wants to reach.* A culture that had never heard of witchcraft would find Lutz's metaphor unintelligible. Similarly, a culture in which witchcraft was, in fact, practiced widely could find the rather humorous way in which Lutz frames his metaphor to be disrespectful or arrogant.

DESCRIBE THE FUNCTIONS OR ORGANIZATIONAL STRUCTURE OF A GROUP

Ethnographers can follow the tenets of functional theorists, beginning with a description of the whole society or culture in terms of its functions or structural organization.

━━•━━•━━ **EXAMPLE 10.9**

BEGINNING WITH A FUNCTIONAL DESCRIPTION

Hostetler and Huntington (1971) studied the Amish, a religious community in the United States that follows practices of simple rural living, shuns modern urban technology, and adheres to Protestant Christian beliefs and practices generated in the 1800s. Treating the Amish as a tribe, or self-contained culture, the researchers examined each aspect of the community's life—family, farming, schooling, religion, and so on—in terms of its relationship with other components of Amish culture and its contribution to the overall harmony and survival of Amish life. The goals of education, for example, were to impart literacy sufficient to read the Bible and to engage in general commerce and agricultural life as the Amish practiced it. The Amish felt that 8 years of formal schooling were sufficient, and they tended to set up their own schools if they viewed teachings in the public schools in their areas to be detrimental to their beliefs. Thus, schooling supported their traditional lifestyle; it was not designed to expose the Amish to other cultures and ways of living, nor to encourage them to leave their own community. The Amish, in fact, have a long history of litigation against requirements that they send their children to school for longer than the 8 years they feel sufficient for their needs, or to schools whose instruction is inimical, in their view, to their religious teachings.

━━•━━•━━

A functional or structural analysis such as Hostetler's and Huntington's identifies the basic components in the community, group, or culture and then describes the operations of each. Further analysis can address how the components support or interfere with each other, and what the consequences of these relationships are for life within the community and its relationships with external groups and influences.

WRITE UP THE CRITICAL EVENTS
IN CHRONOLOGICAL ORDER

Ethnographers often begin by describing a series of critical events that have occurred during the course of fieldwork, linking these together in chronological fashion. These descriptions of a temporal, usually passing, reality can form the beginnings of a narrative, as is the case of the faculty meeting depicted in Example 10.6. In her report, LeCompte created vignettes of several other critical events, including the decisions of the first principal and a key arts teacher to resign, and a town meeting in which the community changed its mind about closing the school in which Arts Focus was located. These critical elements or events formed the focal points around which the remainder of the report was written.

MAKE A LIST OF THE MOST
IMPORTANT EMPIRICAL FACTS

Sometimes, the most important results from a study involve a catalog, dictionary, or encyclopedia of empirical facts. These can include an ordered listing of vocabulary in a language or for a professional field or specialty practice; a taxonomy of behaviors or events, such as all of the types of locations appropriate for placing hospitals, clinics, schools, coffee shops, residential housing, or other institutions; a taxonomy of all of the ways people can contract a communicable disease; or a taxonomy of all of the factors that are associated with students' failure to complete high school. Sometimes, these lists are enough by themselves to constitute a report. At other times, the researcher needs to sit down and write a short narrative describing the most important things he or she believes the research says, continue the write-up by giving reasons why these points are important, and then elaborate on each narrative by providing evidence in support of those reasons.

CREATE A DISPLAY; OR,
WHEN IN DOUBT, DRAW A PICTURE!

With the exception of Vadeboncoeur's conceptual and analytical model diagrams, all of the forms of analysis we have discussed so far involve creating texts. However, this obscures the fact that one of the most important ways of analyzing data involves figuring out how to draw pictures of what you have found. Miles and Huberman (1984) call this the "display" aspect of data analysis; a display is a "spatial format that presents information systematically to the user" (p. 79).

We are accustomed to looking at all kinds of displays; the menus on computer screens and websites on the Internet are displays; so are charts and graphs, diagrams showing how to assemble children's toys, and the gauges on automobile dashboards. Miles and Huberman view display as a central component of analysis, building it into their research sequence (see Figure 10.2). They argue that "you know what you can display" (p. 79)[1] and suggest that presenting analyzed data in narrative text form alone has serious limitations.

First of all, text is dispersed and requires many pages to present what a table can display in one. Many people—especially policymakers and administrators—do not have time to read pages of text, and others find them intimidating. Visually oriented people also find it easier to grasp complex information when it is graphically presented, rather than merely as text. Furthermore, because narrative usually is presented in sequential or chronological form, it is difficult for text accounts to consider three or more variables at once—as Vadeboncoeur's table (Figure 10.1)

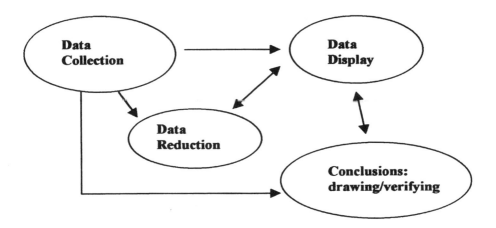

Figure 10.2. Conceptual diagram: Miles and Hubeman (1984).

displaying the development over time of teacher-training students does. Regardless, a display of some kind often permits the researcher to look at many kinds of data simultaneously, in a focused and systematically arranged format. Displays can permit the researcher to show to an audience the actual process or sequence of his or her data collection and analysis strategies, something that often helps to convince skeptical audiences that the work was done in a systematic and rigorous fashion. Displays also give plenty of opportunity for interesting and vivid graphics, which are becoming increasingly easy to create, given software that creates both black-and-white and color graphics on personal computers and programs that permit computers and projectors to be linked for animated presentations.

How to Start Creating a Display

Displays can begin with the simplest of materials: newsprint and self-stick notes (or tags of paper with glued edges that can be pasted in place, moved, and repasted); sheets of paper; scissors; glue; and tape to create large spreadsheets or sketches. Key to thinking about displays is flexibility; the researcher has to be able to move pieces of information around, explore different ways of portraying relationships and connections, and revise constantly. Also necessary is a rather large surface on which to compose and assemble ideas, and paper or drawing material larger than a computer screen or standard letter paper. Ultimately, displays must be reduced to paper, slide, or photo size, but restricting scope in the initial stages also restricts imagination.

Many researchers are tempted to begin creating displays on computers; although the most advanced software graphics can provide much of the flexibility described above, they are expensive, not available to all, and sometimes difficult to transfer to other media. Less sophisticated software tends to enforce two-dimensional, linear, and even boxlike thinking; our bias is that researchers should not start off creating displays on the computer. The Arts Focus conceptual framework involved organizing and reorganizing chunks of data spatially and visually; LeCompte and Holloway began with a pad of $1\frac{1}{2}$-meter by $2\frac{1}{2}$-meter newsprint paper, as well as self-stick notes or stickers in six different colors (to denote different domains) and in large and small sizes (to represent subdomains and sub-subdomains). The categories of data and specific indicators were written on the self-stick notes and then organized on the newsprint sheets. Each large sheet constituted a domain. One specific color of sticker was designated to represent the subdomains within the domain; smaller-sized stickers of the same color represented the subdomains, and the even smaller stickers represented the behaviors that were indicative of the subdomain.

LeCompte spread the sheets of newsprint all over her kitchen and living room tables for several days while she and the research team discussed where various stickers should go. The process moved stickers—and sheets of newsprint—around, sometimes dividing a single sheet into several so that what had appeared to be one domain became subdivided into several separate domains. The physical process of moving, cutting, pasting, and rearranging paper visually reinforced the cognitive process of comparing, contrasting, matching, modifying, and clarifying needed to create not only a viable set of codes for analysis, but also to clarify the conceptual structure of the study overall. Whereas LeCompte found the process described above to be useful in organizing masses of data, paper-and-pencil doodling often is the most appropriate way to begin creating conceptual diagrams, such as those Vadeboncoeur used in her study or some of the kinds of displays described later in this chapter.

Drawing diagrams and abstract representations can be done initially on a computer with a sketch program, but the linear and two-dimensional nature of computers and their logic, as well as the limited size of the computer screen, often constrain flexibility and imagination in the earlier stages of the process. This is why we suggest beginning with paper and pencil or newsprint and stickers.

TYPES OF DISPLAYS

Contrast or Contingency Tables

Contingency or contrast tables are one of the most common types of display. They generally present a way to represent differences between two or more groups on a given dimension; the differences usually are given in numerical data, but they can also be used to show the presence or absence of a trait, practice, or belief. Contingency tables can be used to show, for example, differences between males and females in the percentages that patronize credit unions or attend soccer matches. A 2×2 contingency table also can be used to display data on the economic status of people who are divorced in the United States by sex (see Figure 10.3).

Sex	Economic Status After Divorce
Males	Higher than while married
Females	Lower than while married

Figure 10.3. A contingency table.

A table such as this could be elaborated, displaying the same data for African Americans, Hispanics, European Americans, or Asian Americans and indicating the percentages of males and females of each ethnic group that experience upward and downward mobility.

Event Lists and Time Lines

Event lists simply present a comprehensive list of all of the events or activities that have occurred during a given period without organizing them in any particular way. Such lists can be useful to give a sense of variety; they can also be a precursor for a coding activity that would permit enumeration of the frequency of occurrence of specific kinds of events. A time line, by contrast, arranges such events chronologically. Martinez's normative vignette describing how the day begins at Snow Mountain Elementary School is artful (see Example 10.4), but the entire description of the day requires some 10 pages of text. Another way of presenting "A Day in the Life" is with a time line, as in Figure 10.4. Medina (1998) used this time line to introduce a much longer narrative description of the specific kinds of instruction offered throughout the day.

Matrices and Scatterplots

Matrices and scatterplots permit a researcher to display co-occurrence, or one piece of information in terms of another, such as the number of responses (one piece of information) given by each member of a group of infor-

8:30 am:	Student Arrival
	Students came to the classroom from the cafeteria. Students greeted the teachers and each other. They moved the chairs from the top of the tables. Recitation of Navajo Pledge in Navajo followed by the Pledge of Allegiance in English, then a brief period of silence.
8:45 am:	Spelling and Basal Reading Groups in English
	Ability reading groups: low, middle, high
9:20 am:	"Building Specials" in English
	Rotation of art, music, library, PE, and a computer class
10:15 am:	Morning Recess
10:40 am:	Math Groups and Handwriting in English
	Ability group instruction in high, middle, low, or whole group instruction of new material. Chapter I time; 7 students left the classroom for remedial instruction. Homework "Catch-Up" time.
12:20 pm:	Lunch and Recess
1:05 pm:	Reading in Navajo or English
	Teacher read aloud or students read library books. Oral story time.
1:35 pm:	Journal in English
2:00 pm:	Electives in Navajo
	Classroom electives: Navajo studies, Chaa book, writing, weaving, art. Infrequently, health, social studies
3:00 pm:	End of the School Day (Medina, 1998, p. 97)

Figure 10.4. A time line: A typical day in Room 15.

mants (the second piece of information) (see Figure 10.5). Borgatti's chapter on elicitation techniques makes good use of response matrices in the construction of cultural domains. Scatterplots do much the same thing but require numerical data that can be displayed—or plotted—on the axes of a graph (see Figure 10.6). Vertical axes represent quantities or locations of one kind of data; horizontal axes represent quantities or locations of another kind of data.

Gender		Drinking Frequency Totals		
		Less Than Once a Week	Once a Week or More	Total
Male	Count	21	21	42
	% within Gender	50.0	50.0	100.0
	% within Drinking Frequency	34.4	91.3	50.0
	% of total	25.0	25.0	50.0
Female	Count	40	2	42
	% within Gender	95.2	4.8	100.0
	% within Drinking Frequency	65.6	8.7	50.0
	% of total	47.6	2.4	50.0
Total	Count	61	23	84
	% within Gender	72.6	27.4	100.0
	% within Drinking Frequency	100.0	100.0	100.0
	% of total	72.6	27.4	100.0

Figure 10.5. A matrix (cross-tabulations).

NOTE: This matrix illustrates the arrangement of data in a matrix that examines frequency of drinking by gender in urban adolescents. The total number of youth in this study who report drinking is 84. The figure shows that it is much more common for boys than girls to drink once a week or more. The matrix includes row percentages (reading across within gender) and column percentages (reading down within drinking frequency).

Conceptual Diagrams

Conceptual diagrams permit the researcher to map out and display the conceptual and theoretical relationships and structures that guide their study or that they have discovered in the course of the study. The conceptual diagram in Vadeboncoeur's study (Figure 4.1) was constructed at the beginning of her study to illustrate how she planned to code or chunk her data. The conceptual diagram she created to describe the components in her analysis plan is displayed in Figure 10.1. Conceptual diagrams seldom use numbers; they are a convenient way to portray those kinds of information or studies that are, in Miles and Huberman's words, "messier and thicker than numbers," and therefore not amenable to counting or graphical representation.

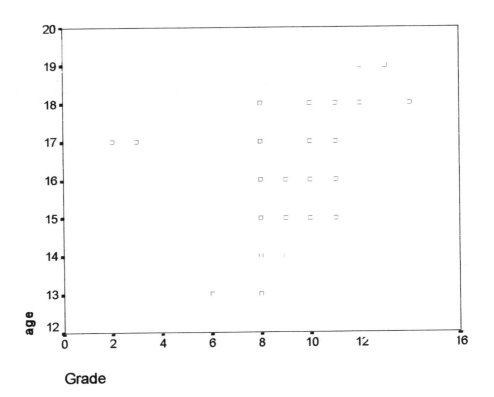

Figure 10.6. A scatterplot.

Taxonomies or Tree Diagrams

Earlier in this chapter, we described how tree diagrams or taxonomies can be used to portray the hierarchical structure of coding and analytic frameworks. Such diagrams also can be used to show the hierarchical arrangement of virtually any phenomenon so organized; a typical kind of taxonomy can be found in the organizational charts of virtually any formal organization.

Taxonomies are usually organized vertically (see Figure 10.7); tree diagrams may be arranged either vertically or horizontally (see Figure 10.8).

1. CHILDREN'S ACTIVITIES
   1.1 Activities: doing things at home
      1.1.1 Sweeping
      1.1.2 Dusting
      1.1.3 Cooking
      1.1.4 Getting groceries
      1.1.5 Washing dishes
      1.1.6 Washing clothes
      1.1.7 Taking garbage out
   1.2 Activities: doing things at school
      1.2.1 Reading
      1.2.2 Writing at desk
      1.2.3 Doing group exercises
      1.2.4 Recess games
      1.2.5 Doing work sheets
   1.3 Activities: doing things after school, at school
      1.3.1 Clubs
      1.3.2 Sports
      1.3.3 Detention
      1.3.4 Tutoring/homework
   1.4 Activities: doing things after school, elsewhere
      1.4.1 Playing in park (not sports)
      1.4.2 Playing outside around the house or on the street
      1.4.3 Going to an after-school program
      1.4.4 Going to the library
      1.4.5 Sports program
      1.4.6 Informal sports with friends
   1.5 Activities: before going to school
      1.5.1 Brushing teeth
      1.5.2 Eating breakfast
      1.5.3 Getting dressed
      1.5.4 Walking to school

Figure 10.7. A taxonomy.

Pie Charts

Pie charts are circular figures that are divided into wedges whose size denotes the relative importance or proportion of components within a single entity (see Figure 10.9). They are often used for displaying such things as the distribution of expenses in a budget, groups within a population, or shades of opinion within a group.

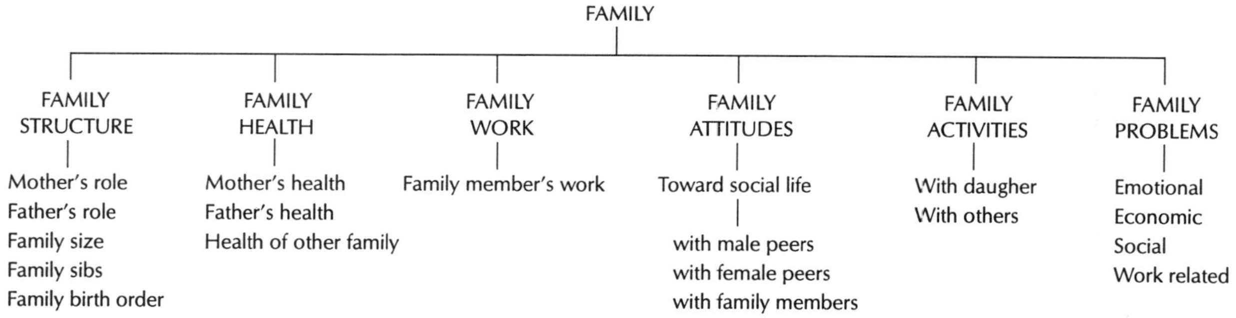

Figure 10.8. A tree diagram.

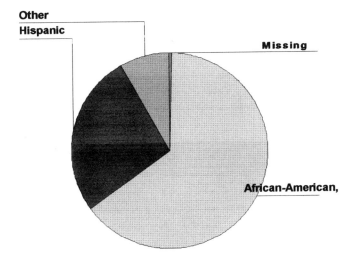

Figure 10.9. A pie chart.

Graphs

Graphs provide a way to represent relative distribution of items. Bar graphs, for example, can display differing amounts of education, drug use, income, or recreational activity among different groups within a population (see Figure 10.10).

Venn Diagrams

Venn diagrams show the overlap among items or concepts in a study. Figure 10.11 displays the three principal forms of teacher behavior that LeCompte identified in her Learning to Work study. Venn diagrams can be presented as overlapping circles, ovals, or other plane figures.

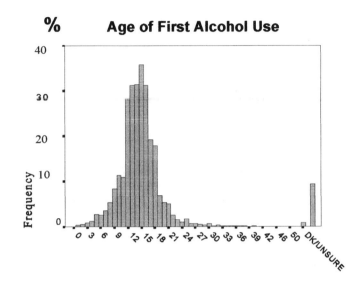

Figure 10.10. A bar graph.

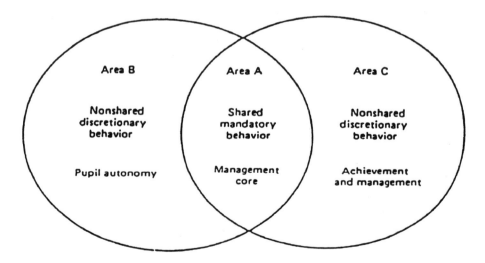

Figure 10.11. A Venn diagram.

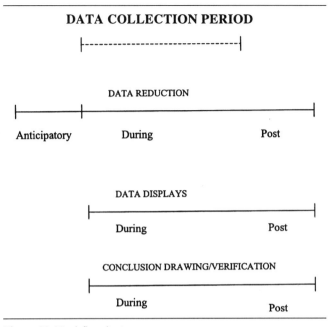

Figure 10.12. A flowchart.

Flowcharts

Flowcharts permit the researcher to portray processes, or the flow of activities over time. They are often used to depict how events transpired, or to assist groups in planning their activities. The research process diagram in Book 1 is such a flowchart, as is the time line in Book 1, Chapter 6. The latter depicts the flow of activities planned for a research project, displayed over the 3-year lifespan of the project. Flowcharts can be organized in many different ways; Figure 10.2 is a flowchart created by Miles and Huberman (1984); Figure 10.12 presents the same material presented in Figure 10.2, but formatted differently.

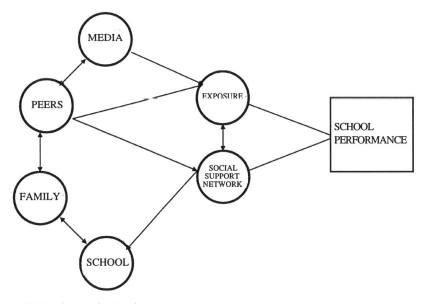

Figure 10.13. A causal network.

Causal Networks

Causal network diagrams resemble flowcharts, but they permit the researcher to order the events, concepts, behaviors, and other components of a cultural scene temporally so as to depict the direction of influences of one on the other. Causal networks portray a chain of events or influences in ways that the researcher expects, or predicts, that they will occur or be related to one another.

Sociograms

Sociograms depict the interaction patterns between individuals or groups of individuals within a particular social setting or context. They are used to show who interacts with whom as well as the relative frequency of interaction among individuals within a group (see Figure 10.14). Sociograms are frequently used in social network research.

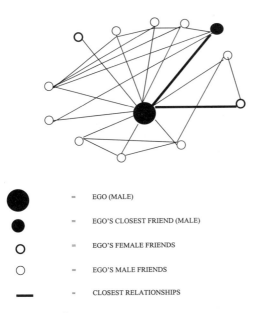

	=	EGO (MALE)
	=	EGO'S CLOSEST FRIEND (MALE)
	=	EGO'S FEMALE FRIENDS
	=	EGO'S MALE FRIENDS
	=	CLOSEST RELATIONSHIPS

Figure 10.14. A sociogram.

In Figure 10.14, the large black circle represents the index person (the start point) who is providing the information about his network. The larger, lighter circles are his immediate male associates. The smaller lighter circles are the close male friends of the index person's immediate associates. The darker circles on the outside upper right and left are "wifeys," or the girlfriends of the index person and of several of his closest male friends. The thinner lines connect associations among individuals in this network. The thicker lines represent drug sales/drug use networks. This sociogram portrays the relationship between the index person and his immediate personal relations. This sociogram provides a great deal of information on the pattern of relationships among individuals, the difference between friendship and drug networks, and the degree to which women partners are excluded from drug exchanges.

As the above discussion and exemplary figures demonstrate, the kinds of displays possible are limited only by the imagination of the researcher! Researchers should remember, however, that many readers are not visually oriented and tend to skip over figures and diagrams, and that even the best diagrams and figures do not always speak completely for themselves. It is important to include a narrative with figures to tell readers what the figure portrays, what they should notice within it, and what the researcher thinks is important about the figure or diagram.

Any of these display tactics can be converted to electronic or nontext formats and augmented with photographs and even documentary films. These methods allow researchers to display their work to larger groups. The simplest forms of visual presentation involve making printed paper handouts or using flip charts, large sheets of newsprint, or an overhead projector to display text-based material. Other formats that require more technical expertise and equipment are slide shows; computer-assisted displays, such as PowerPoint; or combinations of technology using visuals and sound, such as CD-ROMs. These techniques can make even the most arcane of presentations more interesting. However, we hold out several important cautions to researchers desiring to use these methods.

- Do not substitute sophistication of display or technical prowess for excellence of research results. Many researchers become so enamored with their PowerPoint or other computer software capabilities that they spend more time developing presentations than they do analyzing and interpreting data. Thus, although their presentations are wonders of technical razzle-dazzle, they lack substance.

- Remember that equipment always fails. As we have noted in previous chapters and books in this series, expected equipment may not be delivered, or if delivered, it may be broken. Bringing one's own equipment is not always sufficient; it, too, can malfunction. Power cords can be too short to reach outlets,

outlets may be missing altogether, light bulbs can burn out, audiotapes will stick, and computers can develop mysterious fatal ailments. The electricity can go out altogether—just when backup batteries go dead. This is why, although we have become dedicated advocates of high-tech presentations because they can be so effective, we also believe that researchers at all times should have in reserve a foolproof backup that requires no equipment of any kind for success.[2]

SUMMARY

In this chapter, we have discussed how researchers formulate their coded and analyzed qualitative data into meaningful stories and then organize those stories or compilations of data into displays that facilitate the understanding of the various audiences whom the ethnographer wants to reach. In the final chapter, we discuss interpretation of data, or how researchers go about making sense of the results they have obtained and translate that sense into reports, presentations, and documents that are meaningful to research participants, informants, partners, funding agencies, and other external constituencies.

NOTES

1. Another way of phrasing this might be, "If you can display it, you must really know it!"

2. The above list of horror stories is not imaginary; it was compiled from actual situations in which the authors have found themselves!

11

CREATING INTERPRETATIONS

Up to now, we have been talking about the process of crunching data, or turning it from piles of raw or unanalyzed information into results or summarized and succinct reports on what the ethnographer found. These steps in the process have ranged from using preexisting schemes for coding, enumerating, and interpreting data to inductive methods for chunking data and dividing the observed stream of experience into items, bits, and units that can be individually studied and then reassembled in ways that illuminate their contribution to an entire cultural portrait. We also have talked about ways to start telling a story —and then presenting it to readers in comprehensible ways.

All too often, researchers arriving at this stage of the research process believe that their job is finished. *Mere results, however, do not speak for themselves. Researchers must interpret their data.* This means telling the audience— often a number of different kinds of readers with multiple agendas and differing capacities for understanding and making use of research results—just what those results mean. This can be a challenging process, because it means taking leaps beyond the data, or beyond what the crunched results actually portray, to try to set the results in a broader context. Many researchers find it discomforting to depart

Key point

213

from results. But going beyond results is exactly what researchers are trained and hired to do.

Although what all researchers hope to find out is something that nobody else knows, much of what researchers do is illuminate the obvious. Often enough, informants, research participants, research partners, and even funding agencies greet the well-crafted report of an ethnographer with the statement, "Well, but everybody knows that!!" In many ways, the job of the ethnographer is, in fact, to attribute meanings and importance to patterns and regularities that people otherwise take for granted in everyday life—until a researcher points them out, highlights them, and gives them broader significance by associating them with other experiences, situations, and literature.

However, although people in the site might have lay or folk beliefs about what "everybody knows," they are not likely to be able to step back from everyday knowledge to pinpoint the significance or implications of such knowledge for future practice or program innovation. Nor can they see clearly the relationships of the group or institution in question with other groups, or the meaning of the results for the overall survival of each. Finally, they cannot set the work in the context of other research on the same topic. This is because insiders generally do not have the opportunity to read the literature, see similar sites, or compare their situation with others. Locally situated, they do not usually gain the external perspective that researchers have—and that they are hired to provide as part of their presentation of results.

For example, although the teachers in the Arts Focus program appreciated the careful analytic descriptions of their practice that LeCompte and Holloway produced, they were not very surprised at the results. However, when interpreted, these analyses (the results) helped everyone in the school understand the implications that the arts teachers' activities might have for the other teachers on the faculty of Centerline Middle School. They also provided insight as to what those results meant to other arts teachers in the school district and to teachers at Centerline Middle School in general, as Example 10.6 indicates. Interpretations in LeCompte's and Holloway's reports were useful to parents who were trying to choose an appropriate school for their children, and they might also have helped the school board make decisions about which programs to support and which to eliminate because of declining educational funds in the community. Similarly, Schensul et al.'s work in Mauritius (Schensul et al., 1994) and Silva et al.'s work in Sri Lanka (Silva et al., 1997) set research on sexuality and sex risk in the context of rapidly growing AIDS risk in the Indian Ocean area (Schensul, 1996) by demonstrating that the risk factors for promoting HIV infection were present despite low HIV prevalence rates in both countries. At the same time, the research provided support for the importance of promoting national policies favoring sex education as a means of AIDS risk prevention in countries with deeply conservative religious and cultural ideas with regard to sexuality.

Although all of the above constituencies were local, the product of most research projects should not be limited to the immediate community in which the study was done. Results and interpretations from the Arts Focus study, for example, could be of use to curriculum theorists and educational psychologists trying to develop more effective ways to teach children, as well as to museum directors, supporters of the arts, and artists trying to build more support for the arts in their communities. Similarly, research methods and results on sexuality and AIDS risk conducted in two countries in the Indian Ocean area are now being disseminated by Stephen Schensul and colleagues throughout other southeast Asian countries with the support of the World Health Organization and the Rockefeller Foundation. Book 7 is devoted to a discussion of additional ways in which ethnographic research can be used and disseminated in policy, intervention, and public program settings.

Cross Reference: See Book 7 for more information on approaches to disseminating research to policy makers, public programmers, and interventionists

Mere presentation of results cannot provide the kind of guidance that constituencies such as these need to make use of the products of a study. Rather, these products must be carefully interpreted for potential users, whose needs must be identified in advance and used to shape the kind of report produced by the researchers. The strength of the interpretation and any subsequent recommendations that might come from it lies in the skill and integrity with which ethnographers use their results to support the interpretation and the methods of delivery that they devise for their presentation. Furthermore, the methods of presentation should be chosen with reference to the audience that the researcher wants to reach. As the above discussion indicates, there are many possible audiences for this single study of arts education, just as there are many for the studies of HIV risk exposure conducted in Mauritius or Sri Lanka.

In the following box, we describe steps that researchers can take to interpret their data and some of the central considerations and constraints that affect the direction of the interpretation.

Cross Reference:
See Book 7 for chapters on approaches to the dissemination and utilization of ethnographically derived knowledge

---

Strategies for Initiating
Interpretation of Research Results

- Speculate with research partners
- Review the research questions
- Return to the formative ethnographic theory
- Review relevant theories in the field
- Evaluate the program
- Present an "emic" interpretation and then contrast it with other, outsider interpretations
- Repeat the same analytic processes used to generate results
- Look for program relevance
- Look for policy relevance
- Consider the audience

ENGAGE IN SPECULATION

Throughout this book series, we have emphasized the importance of partnership in research and of embedding research in local settings and communities where it has local meaning. Interpretation, like theory building, can be thought of as operating on two levels—local (with research partners) and general (in relation to other studies and the literature on the topic). Although careful researchers often find it difficult to speculate about how their data might be used and the implications that the data might have for theory and practice, it is their job to do so. *An important* first step in getting started is to enlist the help and support of research partners in considering the meaning of the research results to them.* Systematic review of research results with interested partners can have important implications. Partners gain deeper commitment to the results and their use and see new ways of using the research for their own purposes. They also provide important insights to the researchers. The brainstorming and thought that go into speculation, dreaming, and "playing with ideas" (LeCompte & Preissle, 1993) can generate some of the most valuable connections between a current project and those to come.

Key point

REVIEW THE RESEARCH QUESTIONS

A second step can involve reviewing the research questions to identify what initial hunches the researchers might have had about the significance of the study and its connection to existing bodies of research or knowledge. Does the study enhance, confirm, modify, or disconfirm what is already known about the research questions asked? If so, in what ways? Do these confirmations, negations, modifications, or clarifications lead the researchers to revise and reformulate the original research questions? Were they the right ques-

Key point

tions at the right level of abstraction? Most research raises as many questions as it answers. In interpretation, researchers can reframe the original questions. In Jean Schensul's study of Latino children's activity outputs, the original question did not take into consideration gender differences. When she compared the findings of the study to the research literature on the topic, she noticed not only that there were few publications on Latino children's activities, but that what literature did exist did not consider gender differences, either in children activities or in their energy outputs (Schensul, Diaz, & Woolley, 1996). The study question was then revised to consider gender differences in socialization practices and contextual factors playing a role in differential energy outputs.

REVIEW THE FORMATIVE ETHNOGRAPHIC THEORY

Some studies based on prior field research begin with more clearly formulated ethnographic theories; others construct theoretical frameworks in the process of analysis. These frameworks are based on some fairly specific hypotheses or hunches that are tested continuously through preliminary analyses in the field and finalized in the study's analytic phase. The hypotheses or hunches usually are based on both the researcher's growing understanding of circumstances in the field and his or her knowledge of the literature or comparable studies. *In the end, it is important to return to the formative ethnographic theory guiding the study.* If several iterations of the formative theoretical model have emerged during the course of the study, researchers can return to each one and examine the assumptions of each, review how the changes in the model occurred, and explain why the changes were made. Good iterative research involves not only strengthening and enhancing models over time, but continuously interpreting and reinterpreting the

 Key point

meaning of the data. Revising the history of the model as it grows is one way of reconstructing thinking about the data throughout the history of the project. The explanations for why the changes have occurred contribute to interpretation of the meaning of the study.

REVIEW RELEVANT THEORIES

A study is generally based on one or more theoretical approaches or guiding frameworks. *Researchers should begin their interpretation by reviewing relevant theories proposed by other researchers working on the same or related topics.* In what ways does the study confirm, disconfirm, modify, or clarify existing theories explaining what the researcher studied? Because there are many possible theories from which to select, returning to the unit of analysis is helpful here. If the study is about understanding the behavior or attitudes of individuals, for example, then psychosocial or structural theories that predict such behavior can be reviewed. If it is about groups, or units within larger institutions, such as classrooms or clinics, small group or organizational theories can be reviewed. Perhaps the study compares socialization practices in a number of different communities. In this instance, theories about the topic at the community level might be useful to review at the start.

Key point

Cross Reference:
See Book 1, Chapter 5, on choosing populations and units of analysis

To explore how others have used these theoretical viewpoints, researchers can turn to other studies set within the paradigm(s) they originally selected to guide the study. They can also turn to what some have called "midrange theory" (Merton, 1967; Pelto & Pelto, 1978), or grounded or substantive theory (Glaser & Strauss, 1967), which is theory that focuses specifically on explanations of local phenomena in the research site or that help to explain associations at the domain or structural level. Trotter and

Cross Reference:
See Book 1, Chapter 3, for a discussion of research paradigms, and Book 2, Chapter 2, for a review of some ways to think about theory

Schensul (1998) discuss some of the middle-range or substantive theories that social scientists use to explain behavior at the individual and cultural levels, especially in applied work, are the following:

I. Individual level: Sociocognitive Theories
   - Cultural Models Theories
   - Consensus Theories
   - Social Construction Theories
   - Scripting Theories

II. Cultural level: Cultural Contexts Research
   - Social Network Theories
   - Cultural Ecological Theories
   - Critical Theory

Using these types of theories, researchers should ask whether comparisons between their own study results and what others have found and concluded about similar topics confirm, negate, modify, or clarify the study's results. If so, people—even researchers—may have to change what they think about the topic under study. Such modifications may even lead to the emergence of a new theoretical framework.

REPEAT THE ANALYTIC STRATEGIES
THAT PRODUCED RESEARCH RESULTS

 Key point *It sometimes helps the interpretive process to play with ideas and theorize with finished results in the same way one did when the results were being developed.* This involves engaging in the same analytic processes used in creating items, patterns, and structures. Researchers can compare and contrast the study's results with those of other studies; make connections or linkages between what was found in this study and results from similar studies, and try to find theories that explain the results more adequately than current theories. Metaphors, analogies, and similes can help users unfamiliar with the specifics of the research site or project to understand what was found and how it might connect with their own concerns. For example, in the 1970s, researchers who found that decision making in organizations did not follow what they assumed to be logical lines compared the decision-making process to a soccer or basketball game where decisions were made "on the fly" by assessing conditions from moment to moment. From there, they went on to develop a new theory of decision making in organizations and bureaucracies. Similar examples can be found in the examples, cited in this book, of medical research among Cambodian and Hmong populations (Feldman, 1997) and school reform studies (LeCompte & McLaughlin, 1994).

PRESENT A CONTRASTED INSIDER AND OUTSIDER PERSPECTIVE

Researchers can begin by presenting the data as participants in the study interpret them, which constitutes an emic, or insider's, approach. They can then contrast this emic presentation with the way outsiders would view the same data (cf. Pelto & Pelto, 1978, pp. 54-65). We note research of this type elsewhere in the **Ethnographer's Toolkit**.

Key point

Cross Reference: Distinctions between insider, or emic, and outsider, or etic, approaches or perspectives are presented in Books 1 and 2

LOOK FOR PROGRAM RELEVANCE

Part of the interpretation also can address the extent to which a study's data and research questions were relevant to the group, program, or organization it studied. It is particularly important to look for program relevance when at least one component of the study involves an evaluation. Did the study enhance program objectives? If so, in what ways? If not, why? Were there unintended consequences or surprise

Key point

results? If so, what might have accounted for them? Did the research provide data that program participants could use? Why or why not? Interpretation involves

- Describing the differences between the expected and the observed
- Explaining these differences both from an emic perspective and through comparison with other researchers' results for similar projects
- Discussing implications for the project in question and for work in the field addressed by the program

In Chapter 1 of Book 7, authors Nastasi and Berg discuss the ways in which ethnographic research can inform programs at the formative, implementation, and outcome stages.

LOOK FOR POLICY RELEVANCE

Key point *Interpretations also can address policy relevance.* Sometimes, a study specifically focuses on a policy-related question. Examples of policy-related questions guiding research are the following: "What models of transitional housing for women are more likely to result in social and economic independence?" "Should the Houston Board of Education (or any other board of education) implement an arts and education program such as Arts Focus on a larger scale?" or, "Has decentralization resulted in improvements in educational outcomes in the Chicago public schools?" Other research may not be specifically policy oriented but may have implications for decisions under consideration by policymakers. The study of third- and fourth-grade children's activity outputs, for example, was never intended to be a policy research study. But in light of decisions made to increase physical education programs in the Hartford public schools, it had important implications for decisions regarding the types of programs needed for girls and boys at that grade level.

Researchers should address whatever light the study's results shed on current public or private policy governing the groups, programs, or organizations that were the target of the study. To base interpretations on policy requires that researchers spend some time reading the appropriate literature, including newspapers, and talking with policymakers to know which policy decisions are current and how to frame results in order to ensure that they are recognized as important.

Cross Reference: See Book 7, Hess's chapter on using ethnographic research to improve policy making

EVALUATE THE PROJECT

Often, a study is commissioned as a straightforward evaluation. In such cases, *interpretation of data must address whether or not the project under study met its own objectives and, if so (or if not), why.* Here, interpretation rests on an explanation of these results. Evaluation also can ask whether or not those objectives were adequate or whether they were so narrowly construed that they did not really address the bigger goals of which the project was a part. Interpretation then can address the reasons for the disjuncture and focus readers on implications of the results for the project, for the context within which it is set, and for other projects like it. Some of the same considerations apply here as to interpretation for program relevance.

Key point

Evaluation is a politically charged activity that often involves making decisions about whether a program should be continued, changed, expanded, or discontinued. Insofar as it has the power to influence policies—and indeed, sometimes is commissioned specifically because it is intended to influence a policy regarding the program in question—it may be considered to be policy research. Researchers should study the political context of the evaluation, both while they are conducting it and afterward, to know how to frame their results.

CONSIDER THE AUDIENCE

Key point *Interpretations also should take into consideration what audiences need to hear.* Audience issues address not only what significance or implications the data might have but what data to present and how to present them. To some extent, this means deciding at what level of specificity or abstractness the presentation should be. For example, an interpretation that focused on the positive impact of the arts program on the teacher morale, student achievement, and school climate might be most useful to teachers; such a report could help them have the confidence to plan ways to integrate the arts throughout all content areas taught in the school. However, the principal might need an interpretation that used the same data but focused on the value of the arts to children's cognition and success in school overall to convince a skeptical school board to provide sufficient funds for the program. Arts administrators, by contrast, would be more interested in the extent to which such programs could be expanded to reach more children—future patrons and consumers of the arts—so as to convince them about the value of participation in the arts. As for policymakers, proper interpretation requires knowing enough about the different audiences to whom the research results are targeted to know how to organize and present those results so that they will be meaningful as well as heard.

SUMMARY

In this book, we have described strategies for interpreting a body of research results in ways that are meaningful both to the research community and to a variety of lay constituencies. These strategies are used in the last stage of the research process; they involve spelling out the significance of the findings for any number of users in the local community or organization sponsoring the research, for funding agencies, the researcher's own professional and disciplinary peers, policy-oriented agencies, and even governmental bodies. Often, interpretations for differing audiences must address different segments of the research results, or present them in different ways, because information needs for each group seldom will be identical. For a discussion of how and with whom researchers collaborate in the field and the types of information needs that such collaboration generates, we refer readers to Book 6 of the **Ethnographer's Toolkit,** *Researcher Roles and Research Partnerships.* In addition, Book 7, *Using Ethnographic Data,* presents a series of case studies showing how ethnographic data are used in public programming, policy analysis and implementation, and intervention programs.

REFERENCES

Apple, M. W. (1995). The NCTM standards as a slogan system. *Journal of Research in Mathematics Education, 23,* 412-431.

Babbie, E. (1995). *The practice of social research* (7th ed.). New York: Wadsworth.

Bernard, H. R. (1995). *Research methods in anthropology: Qualitative and quantitative approaches* (2nd ed.). Walnut Creek, CA: AltaMira.

Broomhall, L., Wilson, D. S., & Singer, M. (1998, December). *I don't steal: Reconciling contradictions in the reporting of sensitive information by heroin and cocaine users.* Paper presented at the American Anthropological Association meetings, Philadelphia.

Brouillette, L. (1996). *A geology of school reform.* Albany: State University of New York Press.

Clifford, J. (1990). Notes on (field)notes. In R. Sanjek (Ed.), *Fieldnotes: The making of anthropology* (pp. 47-71). Ithaca, NY: Cornell University Press.

Cohen, J., & Cohen, P. (1983). *Applied multiple regression/correlation analysis for the behavioral sciences.* Hillside, NJ: Lawrence Erlbaum.

Fadiman, A. (1997). *The spirit catches you and you fall down: A Hmong child, her American doctors, and the collision of two cultures.* New York: Farrar, Straus and Giroux.

Friedenberg, E. Z. (1970). Curriculum as educational process: The middle class against itself. In *The unstudied curriculum: Its impact on children.* Overly, NV: ASCD Elementary Education Council, and Washington, DC: The National Educational Association.

Geertz, C. (1973). *The interpretation of cultures: Selected essays.* New York: Basic Books.

Gilligan, C. (1982). *In a different voice: Psychological theory and women's development.* Cambridge, MA: Harvard University Press.

Gilligan, C., Lyons, N. P., & Hanmer, T. J. (Eds.). (1990). *Making connections: The relational worlds of adolescent girls at Emma Willard School.* Cambridge, MA: Harvard University Press.

Gilligan, C., Taylor, J. M., & Sullivan, A. M. (1995). *Between voice and silence: Women and girls, race and relationship.* Cambridge, MA: Harvard University Press.

Glaser, B., & Strauss, A. L. (1965). *Awareness of dying.* Chicago: Aldine.

Glaser, B., & Strauss, A. L. (1967). *The discovery of grounded theory: Strategies for qualitative research.* Chicago: Aldine.

Goetz, J. P., & LeCompte, M. D. (1981). Ethnographic research and the problem of data reduction: What do I do with the 5 drawers and fieldnotes. *Anthropology and Education Quarterly, 12*(1), 51-70.

Gonzales, M. L., Barrera, V., Guarnaccia, P., & Schensul, S. (1982). "La Operacion": An analysis of sterilization in a Puerto Rican community in Connecticut (Hispanic Research Center Monograph Series #7, pp. 47-62). Hartford, CT: Hispanic Health Council.

Holley, F. M., & Doss, D. A. (1983). *Momma got tired of takin' care of my baby.* Publication #82.44. Austin, TX: Austin Independent School District, Office of Research and Evaluation.

Hostetler, J. A., & Huntington, G. E. (1971). *Children in Amish society: Socialization and community education.* New York: Holt, Rinehart & Winston.

Jackson, P. (1968). *Life in classrooms.* New York: Holt, Rinehart & Winston.

Jaeger, R. (1990). *Statistics: A spectator sport* (2nd ed.). Newbury Park, CA: Sage.

LeCompte, M. D. (1974). *Institutional constraints on teacher styles and the development of student work norms.* Unpublished doctoral dissertation, Department of Education and the Social Order, University of Chicago.

LeCompte, M. D. (1978). Learning to work. *Anthropology and Education Quarterly, 9,* 22-37.

LeCompte, M. D., Aguilera, D. E., Fordemwalt, B. E., Wilks, S., & Wiertelak, M. E. (1996). Final report for The Learning Circle, Osborn School District, Phoenix, AZ.

LeCompte, M. D., & Bennett de Marrais, K. (1992). The disempowering of empowerment. *Educational Foundations, 6*(3), 5-33.

LeCompte, M. D., & Dworkin, A. G. (1991). *Giving up on school: Teacher burnout and student dropout.* Newbury Park, CA: Corwin Press.

LeCompte, M. D., & Holloway, D. L. (1997). First year report for the Arts Focus Program, Centerline Middle School, Mountain States School District (pseudonyms).

LeCompte, M. D., & McLaughlin, D. E. (1994). Witchcraft and blessings, science and rationality. In A. Gitlin (Ed.), *Power and method.* New York: Routledge.

LeCompte, M. D., & Preissle, J., with Tesch, R. (1993). *Ethnography and qualitative design in educational research* (2nd ed.). San Diego, CA: Academic Press.

LeCompte, M. D., & Wiertelak, M. E. (1994, April). *Constructing the appearance of reform.* Paper presented at the annual meetings of the American Educational Research Association, Chicago.

Lofland, J. (1971). *Analyzing social settings: A guide to qualitative observation.* Belmont, CA: Wadsworth.

Lofland, J., & Lofland, L. (1984). *Analyzing social settings: A guide to qualitative observation* (2nd ed.). Belmont, CA: Wadsworth.

Martinez, E. L. (1998). *Valuing our differences: Contextual interaction factors that affect the academic achievement of Latino immigrant children in a K-5 elementary school*. Unpublished doctoral dissertation, School of Education, University of Colorado, Boulder.

Medina, B. M. (1998). *Din'e Keh'go Na'anitin: Education in the Navajo way*. Unpublished doctoral dissertation, School of Education, University of Colorado, Boulder.

Merton, R. K. (1967). *On theoretical sociology: Five essays old and new*. New York: Free Press.

Metz, M. H. (1978). *Classrooms and corridors: The crisis of authority in desegregated secondary schools*. Berkeley: University of California Press.

Miles, M. B., & Huberman, A. M. (1984). *Qualitative data analysis: A sourcebook of new methods*. Beverly Hills, CA: Sage.

Mishler, E. (1986). *Research interviewing: Context and narrative*. Cambridge, MA: Harvard University Press.

Murdock, G. P. (1971). *Outline of cultural materials* (4th rev. ed., 5th printing, with modifications). New Haven, CT: Human Relations Area Files.

Nastasi, B., Schensul, J., de Silva, M. W. A., Varjas, K., Silva, K. T., Ratnayake, P., & Schensul, S. (1998-1999). Community based sexual risk prevention program for Sri Lankan youth: Influencing sexual risk decision. *International Quarterly of Community Health Education, 18*(1), 139-154.

NUD•IST 3.0. (1995). Melbourne, Australia: Qualitative Solutions and Research Pty, Ltd.

Patton, M. Q. (1987). *Qualitative evaluation methods*. Newbury Park, CA: Sage.

Pelto, P. J., & Pelto, G. (1978). *Anthropological research: The structure of inquiry*. New York: Cambridge University Press.

Pelto, P. J., Schensul, J., & Yoshida, R. (1978). The principal and special education placement. *National Elementary Principal, 8*(1), 1-6.

Radda, K., Schensul, J., Clair, S., & Weeks, M. (1998, December). *Social security: High risk sites and the context of illicit drug use among older adults*. Paper presented at the annual meetings of the American Anthropological Association, Philadelphia.

Romagnano, L. S. (1991). *Managing the dilemmas of change: A case study of two ninth grade general mathematics teachers*. Unpublished doctoral dissertation, School of Education, University of Colorado, Boulder.

Romero, M. J., & Berg, M. (1998, July). *Indicators and precursors of alcohol use in preadolescent girls: A preliminary analysis*. Paper presented at the annual Cross-site Evaluation Conference, Center for Substance Abuse Prevention.

Said, E. (1978). *Orientalism*. New York: Pantheon.

Sanjek, R. (1990). A vocabulary for fieldnotes. In R. Sanjek (Ed.), *Fieldnotes: The making of anthropology* (pp. 92-139). Ithaca, NY: Cornell University Press.

Schensul, J. (1994, September). *Using qualitative data to validate survey data in assessing AIDS risk in unmarried Mauritian women in the workforce*. Paper presented at the annual meeting of the American Public Health Association, Washington, DC.

Schensul, J. (1996). *AIDS in the Indian Ocean area.* Paper presented at the annual meetings of the American Anthropological Association, Washington, DC.

Schensul, J. (in press). Learning about sex from urban youth. *International Quarterly of Community Health Education.*

Schensul, J., Diaz, N., & Woolley, S. (1996). *Measuring activity levels of Puerto Rican children.* Paper presented at the second annual conferences of the National Puerto Rican Studies Association, San Juan, PR.

Schensul, S., Munoz-Laboy, M., & Bojko, M. (1998, December). *Using national data sets to guide ethnographic research on children and youth.* Paper presented at the annual meetings of the American Anthropological Association, Philadelphia, PA.

Schensul, S., Oodit, G., Schensul, J., Seebuluck, S., Bhowon, U., Aukhojee, J. P., Rogobut, S., Koye Wat, B. L., & Affock, S. (1994). *Young women, work and AIDS-related risk behavior in Mauritius.* Women and AIDS Research Program Research Report Series No. 2 (pp. 86-128). Washington, DC: International Center for Research on Women.

Schensul, S., Schensul, J., & Oodit, G. (1995). *Young women, work and AIDS-related risk behavior in Mauritius.* Phase I Research Report Series, No. 2. Washington, DC: International Center for Research on Women, Women and AIDS Research Program.

Silva, K. A., Lewis, J., & Sivayoganathan, C. (1996). Love, sex and peer activity in a sample of youth in Sri Lanka. In S. Schensul et al. (Eds.), *Youth and sexual risk in Sri Lanka.* Kandy, Sri Lanka: Center for International Community Health Studies, University of Connecticut and Center for Intersectoral Community Health Studies.

Silva, K., Schensul, S., Schensul, J., Nastasi, B., de Silva, M. W. A., Sivayoganathan, C., Ratnayake, P., Wedisingnhe, P., Lewis, J., Eisenberg, M., & Aponso, H. (1997). *Youth and sexual risk in Sri Lanka.* Women and AIDS Research Program Research Report Series No. 2. Washington, DC: International Center for Research on Women.

Siskind, J. (1973). *To hunt in the morning.* New York: Oxford University Press.

Spivak, G. C. (1988). Can the subaltern speak? In C. Nelson & L. Grossberg (Eds.), *Marxism and the interpretation of culture* (pp. 280-316). Urbana: University of Illinois Press.

Spradley, J. P. (1979). *The ethnographic interview.* New York: Holt, Rinehart & Winston.

Tesch, R. (1993). Personal computers in qualitative research. In M. D. LeCompte & J. Preissle, with R. Tesch, *Ethnography and qualitative design in educational research* (pp. 279-314). San Diego, CA: Academic Press.

Trinh, M. T. T. (1989). *Woman, native, other: Writing postcoloniality and feminism.* Bloomington: Indiana University Press.

Trotter, R., & Schensul, J. (1998). Research methods in applied anthropology. In H. R. Bernard (Ed.), *Handbook of methods in cultural anthropology* (pp. 691-736). Walnut Creek, CA: AltaMira.

Vadeboncoeur, J. A. (1998). *Emancipatory knowledge construction in teacher education: Developing critically conscious roles through metaphor and service learning.* Unpublished doctoral dissertation, School of Education, University of Colorado, Boulder.

Van Maanen, J. (1988). *Tales of the field: On writing ethnography.* Chicago: University of Chicago Press.

Von Gunten, K. (1999). *Ways of learning and knowing in Lakota oral stories.* Unpublished doctoral dissertation, School of Education, University of Colorado, Boulder.

Vygotsky, L. (1971). *The psychology of art.* Cambridge, MA: MIT Press. (original work published in 1934)

Vygotsky, L. (1962). *Thought and language.* E. Hanfmann & G. Vakar (Trans. and eds.) Cambridge, MA: MIT Press. (original work published in 1934)

Webb, E. J., Campbell, D. T., Schwartz, R. D., & Sechrest, L. (1966). *Unobtrusive measures: Nonreactive research in the social sciences.* Chicago: McNally.

Weitzman, E., & Miles, M. (1994). *Computer programs for qualitative data analysis.* Thousand Oaks, CA: Sage.

Weller, S. C., & Romney, A. K. (1988). *Systematic data collection.* Newbury Park, CA: Sage.

Wolcott, H. (1990). *Writing up ethnographic research.* Newbury Park, CA: Sage.

Znaniecki, F. (1930). *The Polish peasant in America and the Old World.* New York: Farrar and Rinehart.

INDEX

ABOUT THE EDITORS, AUTHORS, AND ARTISTS

Margaret D. LeCompte is Professor of Education and Sociology in the School of Education, University of Colorado at Boulder. After completing her MA and PhD at the University of Chicago, she taught at the University of Houston and the University of Cincinnati, with visiting appointments at the University of North Dakota and the Universidad de Monterrey, Mexico. She also served as Executive Director for Research and Evaluation for the Houston public schools. In addition to many articles and book chapters, she cowrote *Ethnography and Qualitative Design in Educational Research* and coedited *The Handbook of Qualitative Research in Education,* the first textbook and first handbook, respectively, on ethnographic and qualitative methods in education. As a researcher, evaluator, and consultant to school districts, museums, and universities, she has published studies of dropouts, artistic and gifted students, school reform efforts, and the impact of strip mining on the social environment of rural communities. Fluent in Spanish, she is deeply interested in the education of language and

ethnic minority children. She is a Past President of the Council on Anthropology and Education of the American Anthropology Association and as a Peace Corps volunteer in the Somali Republic from 1965 to 1967.

Jean J. Schensul is a medical/educational anthropologist. After completing her M.A. and Ph.D. at the University of Minnesota, she conducted intervention research in education at the Institute for Juvenile Research and Center for New Schools in Chicago. She served as co-founder and research director of the Hispanic Health Council in Hartford for ten years, and, since 1987, has been founder and executive director of the Institute for Community Research, based in Hartford, Connecticut, and dedicated to community-based partnership research. She has extensive experience in the use of ethnographic and survey research methods in the United States, Latin America, Southeast Asia, China, and West Africa. Her substantive interests are diverse, reflecting the contributions of ethnography to health, education, the arts, and community development. She co-edited three special journal issues on applied research in education, and policy, and, with Don Stull, a book titled *Collaborative Research and Social Change: Applied Anthropology in Action,* and has published on other topics including substance abuse prevention, AIDS, adolescent development, chronic health problems, and the arts and community building. She is the recipient of a number of National Institute of Health Research grants, immediate past president of the Society for Applied Anthropology, former president of the Council on Anthropology and Education, and recipient (with Stephen Schensul) of the Kimball Award for Public Policy Research in Anthropology. She is Adjunct Professor of Anthropology at the University of Connecticut and Senior Fellow, Department of Psychology, Yale University.

Ed Johnetta Miller is a weaver/silk painter/gallery cura-
tor/quilter and Master Teaching Artist. Her work has appeared in the *New York Times* and *FiberArts Magazine* and
in the Renwick Gallery of the Smithsonian, American Crafts
Museum, and Wadsworth Atheneum. She is the Director of
OPUS, Inc., Co-Director of the Hartford Artisans Center,
and consultant to Aid to Artisans, Ghana. She teaches work-
shops on weaving, silk painting, and quilting to children
and adults throughout the United States.

Graciela Quiñones Rodriguez is a folk artist, carving
higueras (gourds) and working in clay, wood, and litho-
graphs with symbols and icons derived from Taino and
other indigenous art forms. She builds *cuatros, tiples,* and
other Puerto Rican folk instruments guided by the inspira-
tion of her grandfather Lile and her uncle Nando who first
introduced her to Puerto Rican cultural history and Taino
culture and motifs. Her work has been exhibited in major
galleries and universities throughout Connecticut, at the
Bridgeport Public Library, and at the Smithsonian Institution.